T0160195

influencer and champion for women through fashion. Her exquisite designs and feminine aesthetic were brought to life in Houston with her passion for personal branding. She has an innate ability to connect with the customer with her very real and relevant approach to fashion. Fotini is smart, talented, inspiring, and a lovely friend."

JULIE ROBERTS

owner of Elizabeth Anthony Boutique in Houston, Texas

"Working with Fotini was a joy due simply to her honesty and humbleness, yet at the same time mixed with her ambition and drive to get to where she wanted to go. I remember, of course, the fears and concerns—especially in the beginning—which illustrate her humbleness but also her strength, drive, and ambition not to give up. She wanted something that, at the time, seemed so far away, but Fotini was always honest about what she did and didn't want, and she is strong in a world that—whether we see it or not—is often controlled by men."

GABRIO CANTINI

president, Cantini International

"From the moment I slip into a FOTINI dress, I feel empowered and effortlessly chic, reminding me to stride into the room standing tall and feeling confident as I feel my best self. I am a believer!"

DANA BANNER LANDOW

attorney, mother, philanthropist

ALTERATIONS *in* LIFE

ALTERATIONS *in* LIFE

Finding My Way in Fashion

FOTINI COPELAND

Published by Advantage, Charleston, South Carolina.
Member of Advantage Media Group.

ADVANTAGE is a registered trademark, and the Advantage colophon is a trademark of Advantage Media Group, Inc.

Printed in the United States of America.

10 9 8 7 6 5 4 3 2 1

ISBN: 978-1-64225-121-0
LCCN: 2019910945

Book design by Carly Blake.

This publication is designed to provide accurate and authoritative information in regard to the subject matter covered. It is sold with the understanding that the publisher is not engaged in rendering legal, accounting, or other professional services. If legal advice or other expert assistance is required, the services of a competent professional person should be sought.

Advantage Media Group is proud to be a part of the Tree Neutral® program. Tree Neutral offsets the number of trees consumed in the production and printing of this book by taking proactive steps such as planting trees in direct proportion to the number of trees used to print books. To learn more about Tree Neutral, please visit **www.treeneutral.com**.

Advantage Media Group is a publisher of business, self-improvement, and professional development books and online learning. We help entrepreneurs, business leaders, and professionals share their Stories, Passion, and Knowledge to help others Learn & Grow. Do you have a manuscript or book idea that you would like us to consider for publishing? Please visit **advantagefamily.com** or call **1.866.775.1696**.

*To the little girl in all of us, struggling to find her voice;
to women around the world, searching for the confidence to
take the leap; and to my readers everywhere: this is for you.
Be bold. Be brave. Be you. You can do it.*

CONTENTS

A Collaboration on the Role of Fashion

You are the influencer of your personal brand.
—FOTINI

s I eagerly wait to be introduced, I feel jitters of anticipation and excitement. I peek from behind the curtain, at the rows of women seated before me in this intimate environment. I feel honored to be here and thankful to share my journey and knowledge and listen to theirs. When I look out at them, I see a diverse group—women of different ages who have varied backgrounds and lifestyles. The one thing I know they share is the desire to invest in themselves. These are successful corporate executives, mothers, philanthropists, socialites, or young women who are entering the business world and want to know how to do it in the best possible way.

Take Lynn, for example. She sits up close and takes notes, listening carefully. When she speaks, she shares her concerns. Lynn is the successful founder and CEO of a small advertising agency, but now that she's in her fifties, she would like to elevate her look, develop a more modern and fashion-forward personal brand to freshen things up. She knows that she is her brand and that the impression she makes on clients and potential clients is vital in preserving the growth of her business.

Or there's Cassandra, a young Ivy League graduate who has been climbing the corporate ladder and has aspirations of running for office. She wonders if her dress-for-success suits have taken her femininity out of the picture and left her looking too stuffy, bland, and unapproachable at first glance.

Or Lauren, recently single and reentering the workforce, who wants to be taken seriously in business while delivering the right message in the dating world.

I understand and identify with every woman here. They have come to me to seek my counsel, just as I once sought the counsel of others. There's a difference, of course. I was finding my way in fashion as a designer; these women are finding their way or wanting to enhance their personal brand through fashion. Whether studying corsetry or fabrics with Italian masters, carefully listening to the words of my production houses, leads, or meticulously arranging mood boards to reflect the vision that had been spinning around in my mind for the next collection, I found my way. Much as a composer will hear a recurrent tune that then becomes a concerto. I learned how to seek inspiration in history books, personal travel experiences, and memories of glamorous women from my childhood.

Fashion will always be my first love. To me, it is as alluring, distinctive, and original as the greatest art. Fashion isn't simply wearable art, though. It offers an opportunity for self-expression in a unique and personal way, because it expresses the visual identity of the wearer as much as the designer. As an extension of the FOTINI fashion brand, my new business serves to assist women in designing their personal brand. As a personal brand enhancement consultant and style strategist, I work with women to tell their story. Together we identify, develop, and implement an enriched and satisfying strategy to achieve their personal goals through style, fashion, demeanor, and capability of self-expression. We discuss how they can gain power and confidence through their visual representation. I counsel my clients on finding and establishing their authentic fashion signature: the personal brand identity that makes a statement from the moment a woman passes by or enters a room, saying, "This is who I am."

When I have been asked to do one of my "talk" format discussions or sit on a panel, it is with a "confidante-advisor" mindset rather than as a lecturer. Regardless of the number of audience members, the environment is comfortable, intimate, and never stuffy. As I wait in front of a door or at the side of a stage ready to make my entrance, to talk not *to* but *with* the women who have come to meet and hear me, I focus on my lifetime of knowledge, insights, and hard work. During my talks, I encourage dialogue with my audience. I focus on making it personal, woman-to-woman, as I relate my own experiences, drawing from them the power and inspiration that lets me give every woman present the confidence and information required to find and enhance her personal brand identity.

> *I counsel my clients on finding and establishing their authentic fashion signature: the personal brand identity that makes a statement from the moment a woman passes by or enters a room, saying, "This is who I am."*

A question I like to start with is, "How would you define your personal brand?"

This is often followed by, "What message do you *want* to convey to society through your personal style?"

"We all have a different mirror that is a reflection of what we care about and respect," I tell them. "I want to provide what you need to make whatever impression you wish while always presenting nothing less than your authentic self. Being able to express who you are through fashion is the key to increased confidence and success."

I look around and see Lynn, Cassandra, Lauren, and all the others present waiting as eagerly to hear what I have to say as I wait to hear their stories and questions. I want to hear about their goals and vision of how they want to see themselves.

As a designer of both elegant and casual attire, from regal gowns to tailored shorts, I was always aware of the importance of women dressing both to please themselves and to make the right impression. What is the best first impression? It is always the one you *wish* to make, the one that says something meaningful about who you are. Your wardrobe conveys a message about you. A first and subsequent impression can be heavily influenced by what we wear.

When I was designing each of my five collections and presenting in New York Fashion Week and Houston Fashion Week, it was always—first and foremost—with women in mind. As a woman designing for women, I understood their need for fashion, style, and *wearable* garments. What do I mean by "wearable"? If a woman isn't comfortable in her clothing, that feeling shows and others will see her as anxious or ill at ease. At my trunk shows, my approach was to listen first, to discover what it was she wanted her wardrobe to say about herself. When you truly listen and care about what someone is trying to say through their fashion choices, you discover who that someone is.

There are keys to putting together the best wardrobe for *you*, not just the best in terms of what pieces are in your closet, but in terms of clothing that enhances a woman's personal brand, clothing that makes the wearer feel confident, as well as influences others to have confidence in her.

The design process is one that I love. From the inspiration that triggers the entire collection, to sketching, creating mood boards, choosing fabrics, to fittings—those are just a few steps. What was equally important and satisfying to me was meeting the clients and discussing how we could accomplish the best fit for the FOTINI garment she had chosen or sometimes just about their wardrobe in general. I always wanted to help women be the best version of themselves. I have helped design a complete wedding experience from the aesthetic and theme, to the attire, including selecting and making the floral arrangements. I have been asked to advise on the interior decor of summer homes. This, of course, is partly lifestyle, but what I find most rewarding is helping women achieve their objectives and empowering them, especially through fashion. Even as a little girl, I was the child that other little girls confided in and came to for help.

At my talks, I share my knowledge with my audience. When I decided to take my career to a new level, I knew it had to involve interacting with other women. I loved dressing them, whether they were my own daughters, or strangers I had met five minutes before who had come to a presentation and been swept away by the intricacy of the tailoring, the luxuriousness of the fabrics, or the romance of the designs. Unlike most designers, I loved getting down on the dressing room floor to pin hems myself and make sure any alterations were perfect. And my clients loved that I did this.

It is all too easy to get lost in the frenzy of fashion. My role is to help women navigate and find the route to success through their visual representation. To clearly see and understand what the return on investment (ROI) is when you invest in your appearance, and how it can actualize what you envision is the key, whatever your goals might be. My role is to help women in finding the best path through fashion individuality, one that is perfectly tailored to their selves, their lives, their dreams, and their ambitions.

Your personal brand needs to be consistent, so that it becomes your signature look wherever you may be going.

Every woman must command the "right" attention and make the "right" impression. You are your own celebrity and muse—a niche!

My message is, "I don't want to change you, I want to enhance you." And I do. I want to help every woman I interact with to learn.

HERE ARE SOME OF THE IMPORTANT POINTS I LOVE SHARING:

- how to find confidence in the power of your personal brand

- the importance of the right fit

- the importance of a good seamstress or tailor and how to find one

- how to assess your own body and know what works best on it

- how to enhance your personal brand

- building a personal brand identity that will fit both professional and personal lifestyles

- the dos and don'ts of fashion

- deciphering event attire

- how and why to discard what you haven't worn in two years

- determining the investment pieces every wardrobe must have

- the role of fashion etiquette in every woman's personal brand

- fashion strategies to build your confidence for any occasion

- the easy way to edit and declutter

- techniques for achieving effortless and chic style

I get pleasure every time I think of the tips and skills I can impart to other women and how quickly these can improve their lives. To start with, the basic questions open the door to self-knowledge, causing many women to examine who they are and how they present themselves in a deeper manner than ever before. You could say I was into personal branding before it became a catchphrase and a popular model for enhanced personal and business success. I was always aware of my personal presentation, while determined never to be anyone but who I am. I got to know how women see themselves by seeing them in my designs and understanding what worked and didn't work for them, not only physically but also emotionally.

When I do a talk with a group of women, I ask them to take this deeper look at themselves, their tastes, and their habits. Some people come because they have bought clothing from my line, some because they follow me on social media. Other clients are businesses or associations that want to me to talk to their senior executives or upcoming graduates soon to enter the workforce. A few even say they heard about my new business and understood that their lives, in business and society, would benefit from my expertise. So they come to hear my story, and, sometimes as a surprise to them, are asked to define their own.

We go through an assessment of their fashion aspirations and their absolute boundaries. I encourage everyone to step outside of their comfort level—even if it is on their tippy toes.

People who already recognized the importance of branding in

making a label, product, or company successful have finally come to accept what was always a must for me and for the women I assist: every person also needs branding, in order to choose which clothes are the best match for their lifestyle and aspirations. There is a great deal of talk about influencers nowadays, but in personal branding, the biggest influence is you. You are the source of the input in the process of marketing yourself in your life.

In the pages to come, you will discover how I developed not just the FOTINI brand, or how I learned to navigate and succeed in the challenging world of fashion. You will also see how I evolved and put my love of helping women into this extension of the fashion business. All paths led to this.

The title of this book, *Alterations in Life,* sums up my life thus far. I have remained true to who I am, but I have made changes, alterations, that have made my life a better fit for me. My hope, both in my business and in what I write here, is to help others see the power in making timely alterations as they go along. Through knowing my story and thinking about their own goals and personal brand, I hope to inspire women to follow their own paths in reaching for the stars.

Through knowing my story and thinking about their own goals and personal brand, I hope to inspire women to follow their own paths in reaching for the stars.

My story, like most of yours, includes both struggles and success; hopes and fears; and making alterations that were unconscious, yet purposeful steps that made me who I am. Definite choices that made slight changes in the silhouette of my career and lifestyle. My personal story started in my birthplace, Greece, then to Canada, and then back to Greece, eventually returning to Canada—yes, a lot of moving! In my early childhood, my experiences greatly influenced how I looked at life and at fashion. My career led me in different directions, to Europe and then Manhattan, until it culminated in its first exhilarating yet anxious milestone: the introduction of the first FOTINI collection, a momentous step that led me to where I am today. Please, change into something comfortable, relax, and join me on my elevator ride to the penthouse.

CHAPTER ONE

Pinch Me—Can This Really Be Happening?

She's always a lady, but she never gives a damn.
—DESIGNER FOTINI, DESCRIBING HER IDEAL CUSTOMER
(*TIME*, NEW YORK FASHION WEEK 2011)

As I stepped onto the elevator at the Gramercy Park Hotel, pressing PH as the dark, polished wood-paneled doors slid shut, the butterflies in my stomach reached a fever pitch, rising as I did to the occasion of my first collection's showing.

The penthouse.

Everything about the penthouse was opulent, like a jewel box: the gleaming peacock blue walls, the lush burgundy carpet, the merlot-hued velvet couches placed here and there, the ruby drapes shading bright slices of afternoon sun over the beautiful park far below. It was the moment before the moment: at six o'clock, on September 12, 2011, New York's fashion editors and elite would arrive to view this, my first ready-to-wear collection.

I started the morning like every other day: sitting by the sunny window in my New York City apartment—*did the blue sky look almost surreal just hours ago?* Because even though everything was ordinary, I had my vanilla yogurt, berries, and granola, sprinkled with cinnamon (I sprinkle everything with cinnamon) and sipped my coffee, my eyes returning again and again to the invitation there on the table that reminded me the day would be extraordinary.

It had crisp, white, heavy linen cardstock. Raised typeset in an elegant silver emboss. Even the shape of it: a single lean rectangle with the logo at the top: FOTINI.

And so here I am, just before the elevator doors slide open, and I'm about to make my mark: to put my name to my work. Putting my name to it feels a bit terrifying, no matter how proud I feel.

This is mine.

This is me.

I am this collection and this collection is me.

But as the elevator rises, the nagging insecurities—even ones I didn't know I had—keep whispering in my ears.

What if no one likes my designs?

Was it all worth it?

But there is no turning back now. There's something outrageous—almost audacious—about creating something that starts in my imagination, then making it a reality in the physical world, and expecting others to come see it. Not only to come see it, but to assess it, critique it. The sumptuous, elegant designs I dreamed up in the middle of so many nights are now real, and people are coming to look at the pieces. That morning, every time I looked at the invitation and saw in those silver embossed letters, *FOTINI*, I felt as if I'd somehow stumbled into another universe. An impossible one where my dreams of making my footprint in the fashion world were about to become a reality.

"Inspired by strong and confident women, Fotini Copeland debuted her Fotini Collection in an intimate presentation with delicate lace dresses, ethereal Grecian gowns, flirty sequined skirts and sweet ruffled blouses, all with a romantic yet modern hand."

—*WWD*, 2012 Spring Ready To Wear

The elevator doors slide open, hours before the event, and I find an entire crew stringing cables, hanging sheets on the walls, setting the lights, and testing the music levels. The penthouse will soon be transformed into the stage where I will present my collection. For the first time since I began this venture, I feel as if there is nothing for me to do.

All I can do is wait.

I hate waiting.

I have no idea how the press will respond.

The collection is already here—the pieces steamed perfectly in all their dark beauty, hanging on white hangers with FOTINI in silver on a roller rack, waiting only for the models to bring them to life. Hair and make-up artists set up and I count the shoes and review the accessories, making sure it is clear which model will be wearing what. I have to do something—this collection is a part of me. Counting, checking, labeling. Suddenly, those whispering voices from the elevator return and I'm overwhelmed, caught by a swirl of emotions I didn't anticipate.

What am I doing here?

Do I even belong?

What will the press think?

Can I do this?

In the months spent putting the collection together, there was no time for emotion: the work was nonstop, and I was on top of everything, from choosing the fabrics, to draping the Chantilly lace and silk chiffon, to the final casting decision for each model. I was laser-focused: there was nothing but the work. Everything pent-up was fighting to come out.

> *I was laser-focused: there was nothing but the work. Everything pent-up was fighting to come out.*

Get it together, Fotini—you can't cry now! People are coming!

But the tears flow anyway. I go to a corner of the main room and let myself have my moment. Then, obedient to my inner voice, I pull it together.

Okay! We have a show to put on!

And just like that, Lisa, my sales representative, is the first one to arrive from my immediate team. After Lisa, everyone else arrives on time at a steady pace: my assistant, my casting director, stylists, the rest of my team, and, of course, the models. They are all as essential to me as my vision, as the fabrics that make each piece come to life. No one succeeds in fashion alone, and my team is a testament to that.

The whirlwind had begun. The casting director, taking a cue from the dark opulence of the collection, had advised me on the casting of the models. It was my first show and he'd tried to push me to be a little more "street, minimal, undone" in the presentation, but I was not a "street" designer in my aesthetic. It wasn't that the suggested look of the models was unappealing to me; it was just not FOTINI and a little voice in my head insisted: stay true to your vision. That was what made me different.

She is as feminine as she is strong.

Now, as the models are staged around the room on the chaise lounges, I wonder if the overall look of the presentation matches the vision in my head: *am I overthinking everything?* Like anyone, I would come to learn the lesson of listening to your instinct, of following your gut. This collection was dark, edgy, and ethereal, yet not street in the slightest. I realized in that moment that staying true to myself—as it had all my years growing up in different places—would be essential.

You have to be yourself, as being someone else will never work.

Adrenaline courses through my entire body in those last hours, fuels me to jump in with a hand here, or a direction there, trying to keep an eye on everything at once. The details are coming together and all that remains is that I get dressed. I scan the room for my tailor, who it appears is five minutes late … then ten … then more.

Every designer has a tailor on hand for emergencies and last-minute changes, and I am no different. I'm not worried as much about the collection, seeing how my team and I stayed up into the wee hours ensuring that the garments were at their best and presentation ready. It's my own dress that concerns me. It's the collection's Sophia gown, in cocktail length: a stunning crepe fabric in a brilliant cobalt blue, complete with plunging back and neckline. I step into it and feel the exhilaration of being literally wrapped up in my own creation. It gives me, in a nerve-racking moment, a serene sense of deep confidence. Because I know, without a doubt, that each piece in my collection is a piece I want to wear.

I believe other women will want to wear them, too.

And then? The string tie on the back of the neckline of this glorious dress malfunctions. During our last-minute touches to the collection late last night, my own dress was not our priority, but it certainly is now!

He'll be here, I tell myself with increasing impatience.

And minutes before the show is set to begin, the tailor rushes in, sweating and apologetic, going on about the stress of a difficult celebrity client.

"She's incredibly demanding—she wouldn't let me leave!" he says, breathless. And it turns out this client is one of my idols from the '80s, someone I turned to when I *just wanted to have fun.*

"Well, you have a commitment here as well—a call or update about what was happening would have been professional and courteous," I say crisply. "But enough said—just sew me into this dress and get it fastened!"

He sews my dress up rapidly—I am ready just in time.

And everything is ready. The models, perfectly dressed and in place; my husband and friends, enthusiastic; and my team, excited and proud.

The lights go down.

Stillness fills the air.

I breathe in deeply, then exhale.

The music starts, and I think: *this is it.*

And then the elevator doors open and it all begins.

CHAPTER TWO
Fotini Means Light

Loneliness and yearning to belong often fuels
imagination and creativity, making dreams come true.
—FOTINI

It was the light in everything that transfixed me. The way the Athens moonlight sliced through the nightclub door every time a new couple or group of patrons came in off the street, my grandfather greeting them like regulars, cutting a dashing figure: a slim six-foot-six in his pure white tuxedo jacket and bow tie, his dark pants, shining dome of a head, stylish glasses framing lively eyes. Four years old, I could hardly believe my eyes at the sight of it all— perched as I was atop the glossy black, ebony grand piano almost like a doll in my white organza dress, my matching ankle socks, my hair pulled *tight*, tied with an ever-present bow. How the women's dresses shone like jewels—emerald, sapphire, and ruby—in the smoke-filled Santé cigarette air of the nightclub. Their tiny waists cinched, their gloves to the elbows, elegant hair sprayed just so, their necks and wrists and ears shining with beautiful jewels.

"How are you, *kouklitsa*?" the guests would ask, smiling, happy to see me once again. I was always plopped down unceremoniously by Papou Kosta, who admonished me to stay in one place, a place where he could see me as he went about his duties as maître d'. These were our evenings, just Papou Kosta and me, and I loved them.

"Ready, Fotini?" he'd call across the early evening at home, while my grandmother, Yiayia Katina, looked on with a hint of something in the purse of her lip. Disapproval? Maybe a hint of jealousy? Nevertheless, we'd set out to catch the trolley making its way through the war-ravaged city. The contrast of destruction and grandeur a sight, as we edged into night, skies pinking up behind us. Papou and Yiayia had fled Egypt to start anew here after World War II. I was starting new, too. And so we sat, Papou Kosta and I, side by side, shifting in unison with the other riders through a tangled grid of streets until finally, up ahead: the Athens Hilton. Lit up white as the moon, it seemed to my young eyes a place where anything was possible, where anything might happen.

Many nights I sat sipping ginger ale brought by cocktail waitresses, the tiny ice cubes sparkly and clinking against the glass, taking it all in—the music, the dresses, the scene. I struggled stubbornly to stay awake before finally giving in, curled on the piano's bench, to sleep.

But it wasn't just nights we had. The next thing I'd know, I'd be waking to sunlight—maybe in Yiayia's room, maybe in Papou's—the previous evening's magic faded into day. I never knew in whose bed I'd wake. Sometimes I'd hear Yiayia and Papou quarrelling. But, retired as they were to separate rooms at night, we'd all sleep each night in peace. It was that they never thought to give me my own room in their home, sitting as it was a few steps down from street level—where the high windows offered a view of Athens life—that made me think I was just a visitor there.

Once I dared to ask: "Why am I here?"

Yiayia's answer: "To care for us when we're old."

"Where's my mother?"

"I'm your mother now."

I missed my mother—my real mother—every morning, every night.

The dolls were all I had left of my family: my parents sent money for exquisite, fancy dolls meant not for playing but for admiring. Yiayia and Papou kept them safely tucked in a front hall closet: some to play with, others designated to save for my sister. But even the special ones saved on the shelf I always brought to life in my mind and in my play: they too had a voice. I'd find refuge there, lost in imagination playing with the dolls for hours, a tiny crack of light coming in. The closet even then felt more than private, but like a sanctuary. It was there that I could usually be found as my grand-mother went about her day. Yiayia, her auburn hair coiffed just so, was always perfumed and dressed. She went to the market every day to get fresh bread or other items for our meals—her matching gloves and hat an elegant set. I would have gone to the beach every day if I could, but on the way out, she'd sometimes proclaim, "No beach today."

Papou Kosta—the boss of that partnership, like all Greek men of that time—would counter, in an out-of-earshot whisper, "Slip on your swimsuit under your dress, Fotini."

So off we'd go then, the silky fabric of my suit hidden under another perfect dress, into the gorgeous Athens day. Sometimes it was to the beach, sometimes to a city square. It wasn't just the stylish patrons and cocktail waitresses that I tried to blend in with my old soul, it was bakers of pastries where we'd stop along our way. We'd sit at wrought iron dining sets, while Papou would place his bets on his favorite soccer team and we'd enjoy our treats, pigeons rising up around us at once like drab fireworks. Each city square was like a small world within the big city. Other days we'd hop on the bus and, indeed, head to the beach.

The world of adults was simple to me: a world where it was easy to fit in. Unlike preschool, in that world of adults I adapted, I fit in. That was, after all, how I'd landed here—a tiny girl living with my grandparents in Athens, alone, missing my family.

My parents had met in Athens years before, and it's where both my big sister, Tina, and I were born. But, seeking more work and a better life, my parents moved to Montreal when I was just six months old. My father found swift employment in the hotel business. The men in my family—with their history of opulence, refinement, and prewar wealth—had hospitality in their blood. It would be the first of many moves: in grade two we moved to Toronto; in grade six Regina, Saskatchewan; and in grade twelve we moved back to Toronto! With each city and move, I attended many schools. After a while, it was sink or swim: I chose to swim. And it made me strong.

After arriving in Canada, my parents soon found that to make ends meet they'd both have to work. And so, at three years old, I was enrolled in nursery school, while my mother went to work. Of course, she dressed me in exquisite dresses, my hair tied back in beautiful ribbons bright as the colors in my beloved box of Crayola crayons. My chestnut brown hair was never, ever down. Worse? I didn't speak English. I was a girl apart, a sure recipe for disaster. In my case: bullying.

Pinching. Scratching. Teasing. Pulling hair.

By lunchtime I'd retreat—bruised up, dress torn, a mess—to the little girls' room, pulling my patent leather Mary Janes up under me on the seat. Besides hiding there, the only respite to it all was an easel, given to me by my teachers, in an area set apart from my classmates. I'd dip the wide brush into bright primary paints, filling the ordinary white paper with color, and into that beauty I'd escape. Somehow, I was both an outcast and in my element.

But as dark morning after dark morning piled up with me shaking—not from the terrible cold in an itchy pompom hat and heavy coat, but from fear in the back of my parents' car. The easel was the only possible thing to look forward to, and so my parents decided something had to change. What I didn't know was that, among immigrants of that time, sometimes small children were sent away to the Old Country to be brought up by their grandparents until they were old enough to not require a sitter, returning when they were grade school age. But I was not there yet; preschool scared me, and the children were cruel. So my father made the decision and bought the ticket.

Then he let my mother know.

The next thing I knew I was at the airport holding the manicured hand of a glamorous Olympic Airlines stewardess, her uniform flawless in navy and white, waving at my family as they grew ever smaller behind me in the crowd.

Standing there, I remember looking back at my mother's face, the blonde curl at the end of her bouffant just so, her beauty only marred by the big, heartbroken tears rolling down her cheeks as she saw me go.

> *"Please don't leave me," I said to my mother, before I lost sight of her as I turned to board the flight.*

"Please don't leave me," I said to my mother, before I lost sight of her as I turned to board the flight.

On board, I happily colored with delicious-scented new crayons, making what I thought were beautiful creations. I didn't know it at the time, but I was learning how to be alone, alone with my paints and crayons. Bored, I wandered the smoke-filled aisles, entertaining other passengers, even sitting on some of their laps, reciting sweet bits of memorized poems about singing birds, on the way to my new life.

And in one ten-hour flight across the ocean, my fate was changed.

And so this life in Athens commenced, with the late nights at clubs and days at the bakeries, or playing with my dolls. Some nights, Papou Kosta would stay home and I'd climb up on his lap, glued as he always was to the small black-and-white TV set in the kitchen. It was there we watched a quiet, extraordinary moment to share—the first man to land on the moon.

On days with Papou at the beach, I'd shed my dress and rush into the sea, tiny feet beating the soft sand, silver light reflecting off the surface of water. Knowing my family was somewhere on the other side, an ocean away.

Sometimes I felt lucky when Papou Kosta and Yiayia Katina would take me to see my maternal grandmother, Yiayia Fotini, for whom I'd been named. Tradition said the first and second children in a family were to be named for the paternal grandparents—but I had been named after Yiayia Fotini.

To get to her town, called Kalavryta, we'd take a train ride over the Corinth Canal, a thrilling journey on skinny, skinny tracks, high above the deep azure waters below. I absolutely loved how scary the journey was. I'd perch at the edge of the window, peering down into the abyss, and imagine what would happen if we fell in. But I knew that (just like my trip across the ocean) my journey across the Corinth Canal would deliver me to yet another world, a world apart from the days I'd come to know in Athens.

In Kalavryta, everything was different.

Perched as it was along the right bank of the river Vouraikos, with Mount Erymanthos rising majestically in the west, this was where lush green forests thrived. Impossibly pleasant townspeople greeted you as you passed, and grandmothers acted just the way you'd expect grandmothers should act.

And that included Yiayia Fotini: loving, warm, and kind.

This was where Yiayia Fotini's kitchen filled with the scent of fresh-baked breads and cakes, where her garden was bursting with big red roses, intoxicating. Where lemon and fig trees beckoned and bloomed. Where Mimi, the cat, aloofly—claws drawn—avoided being caught by one curious little girl.

Yiayia Fotini always seemed sad to see me go.

I always wondered why we couldn't stay longer. But my Yiayia Katina's rights as the paternal grandmother eclipsed Yiayia Fotini's say as maternal grandmother, so after a quick visit, we'd be off toward Athens again.

Still I wondered why I couldn't visit longer with Yiayia Fotini. And I wondered even more why there was no Papou Fotini.

What I didn't know then was that my Papou Spiro, my mother's father, had perished in the Massacre of Kalavryta. It was December 13, 1943. The Nazis rounded up every male of the village over the age of twelve, including my grandfather. They marched them to the top of one of the surrounding hills, lined them up, and killed them all in a wretched blast of machine gun fire. My mother, my aunt, and my Yiayia Fotini were escorted away with all the other women and children to a nearby school, where the Nazis locked them in, setting the school afire. But as they clung to one another, sure of impending death and choking on black air, an Italian soldier—unable to stomach the crime—came back and released them all. The same woods that beckoned me on my trips to see Yiayia Fotini had sheltered her and her daughters in escape.

So just like that we'd be back in Papou and Yiayia Katina's Athens kitchen and the thing I wondered most was why the phone on the wall never rang. It caused so many questions to swirl in my four-year-old mind. Because of the expense, my parents couldn't call frequently.

What they could do—hoping to ease their guilt and my loneliness—was send money for the dolls, all of which I adored. But there was one I liked most of all: an American doll. A doll with blonde hair that curled at the ends and a sleeveless pink-and-orange mod-style dress, her white pleated skirt and matching little shoes just so.

Her name was Swingy.

Along with her 45-rpm record, I'd dance with her, singing, "Come on, Swingy, feel the beat, swing your arms and shuffle your feet." I imagined then that we lived in our own world, a fairy-tale world of gem-colored dresses and sparkling jewels. A world where everyone danced, and everyone was beautiful.

I imagined a world made of light.

CHAPTER THREE

Fourth Grade Fashionista

*The excitement of dreams coming true
is beyond the description of words.*

—LAILAH GIFTY AKITA

T hree years later, the time came that I was boarding another flight, holding another flight attendant's well-manicured hand, and as we flew from Athens to Montreal—over the ocean I'd dipped my feet in with Papou Kosta—I was once again walking up and down those smoke-filled aisles, reciting poems and even breaking into song.

And just like that I was reunited with my family.

Once settled in, another September came and I started first grade. Again, I spoke no English, and was thrown into a class where I felt I didn't belong. Day after day, I cried. My despair was so intense that my teacher, Miss Armstrong, would take me by the hand at lunch and bring me with her to staff meetings in the teachers' lounge. I was positively glued to her. To that end (in an effort to solidify her standing as my "school mom") I started sneaking candy bars from home. I'd slide the candy out of my coat pocket and on to her desk, smiling with admiration. And though Miss Armstrong was so kind to me, she eventually called my parents and put an end to my chocolate generosity.

But when I wasn't entertaining passengers on flights over the ocean, or plying my teacher with treats, there was one girl who brought me great solace and joy. She was a fashion icon, a girl who had grown up to be anything she wanted to be. She was Barbie.

My friends had always been dolls. But my favorite doll at this age had lots of friends of her own: there was Barbie's best friend Stacy, and Skipper, and Francie, and Christie. And they could be anything. Barbie was anything and everything. A nurse, a bride, a movie star, a flight attendant, a fashion model. She was even a classic Malibu girl.

Another important girl in my life was my big sister, Tina, who was five years older than I was, and therefore had a more extensive Barbie collection than I did. Sometimes Tina played Barbies with me. Together we would make a tent on the wide balcony of our apartment and bring out all of our dolls to play together, creating a whole new world where anything was possible. We'd get lost for hours, the afternoon sun edging into night, until our parents called us in for dinner.

Barbie was a way for me to create the world as I wished it could be, remembering my time in Greece, admiring those beautifully dressed women at the nightclub.

My devotion to the dolls occasionally got me into trouble—or, rather, my sister sometimes used my love of Barbie to her own ends. One day, Tina was babysitting me while my parents were at work, and she had a brilliant business idea—at least she thought so. I was barely seven and went along.

Tina dressed me in a pretty dress with a satin bow, handed me a fake Red Cross box she'd made out of cardboard, and then sent me door to door, while keeping an eye on me, as I asked for donations. I went dutifully along with the plan, carrying the box with me through the floors of our apartment building.

Knock, knock.

"Hello, will you please give me money for the Red Cross?" I'd ask.

Even though I didn't speak much English, I was taught the necessary, short sales pitch.

Jingle, clink, clink. The money started to pile up slowly but surely.

And as I knocked on door after door asking for donations, the box soon filled with change. I enthusiastically complied for one reason only: Tina had promised me that I could buy a Barbie with my share of the profits.

It worked. When the box was filled with small bills and coins to Tina's satisfaction, off we went with great anticipation and excitement. A skip in our step, we went to a local toy store to purchase our new Barbie dolls. But, as soon as we got home, we got caught.

Some of the residents, out of concern, had reported us. Our parents, displeased, took our dolls away; the money was returned—the whole scam was a bust.

I felt an injustice had been done! I was only a pawn! I should have been allowed to keep my Barbie!

But as I grew older, nothing could deter my love for her: Barbie played an enormous role in the life of my young mind. Whether she was a businesswoman with an office, or (frequently, inexplicably) a bank teller—I was always making her new clothes on my Barbie sewing machine for her many adventures.

Barbie was my first client.

She was also a constant in an ever-changing existence.

After completing first grade in Montreal, it all began—the

constant moving and relocating that would become the driving force of my childhood. We moved to Toronto, and even though we were in the same city, we were constantly pulling up stakes and starting anew. I can't even recall how many homes in Toronto we lived in or how many new schools I started. All I know is that just when I would make friends and started to feel like I belonged, it was time to move again.

I hated it, but I masked my unhappiness. Those were times of masquerading—putting on a smile and keeping your mouth shut. So I would dive in and make friends, sink or swim every time—often overcompensating by pleasing them and not thinking about my own feelings. I just wanted them to like me—it was a way to survive until the next move, when I'd do it all over again.

Though I don't remember how many times we moved in those four years in Toronto, I do remember one home (perhaps the third one) with particular fondness. It was in East York, an area where many Greek immigrants chose to live. Best of all, the house had a big, beautiful veranda. By then I was in second grade and had made some neighborhood friends, but on many days I chose to be by myself. I'd sit on that veranda for hours.

I'd color with my beloved crayons, always gravitating to the metallic shades: copper, silver, and gold.

I'd trace in purple and red and royal blue ink pens intricate designs with my beloved Spirograph.

I'd play with paper dolls and make them clothes.

All while the rain fell, sometimes softly and other times angrily; it would never distract me. I was lost in my creations.

The paper dolls were my first designs; the Spirograph my first prints. Even at that early stage of my life, fashion and art were ever-growing fascinations.

And so, on a magical day in fourth grade, I was amazed when our teacher, Ms. Teperkis—standing at the head of class in her A-line camel skirt, her blouse with a white base and camel polka dots, a scarf tied neatly around her neck—announced, "We're going to study the Roman Empire, and each of you will be assigned a project."

The idea of studying the Roman Empire resonated strongly, being so close to the Greek, in my young mind.

Ms. Teperkis was small but mighty, and everyone wanted to impress her.

As she walked around the room, her short and dark brown hair as neat late in the day as it was the moment she walked in, she told each student what their project would be. In my head, I imagined that the stars aligned and she felt my obsession with fashion, seeing I was such a girly-girl. When she got to my desk, I looked up in anticipation.

"Fotini, you will be covering the history of fashion of the Roman Empire."

I couldn't believe my luck.

"Now, this is a serious assignment that will require extensive research on your part," she said, but I was already aware of this.

Thinking of the hours of poring over encyclopedias, the content and photos making the research come alive. Thinking of my visits to the library, where I would sign out books, taking a heavy pile home to learn the aesthetics of the time for both women and men. I did love the uniform of the gladiators. It was almost like a gift—I could have so easily been assigned war or The Fall, but I got fashion.

How did this fall in my lap? It was meant to be.

I acquired two cardboard bristol boards to create my presentation. Next, I took pictures from books and carefully traced them, then colored them in with my own version of how I thought they should look in beautiful hues. There were togas and gorgeous jewels, but I translated it all through how I thought they should look without losing the essence of the history.

Essentially, these were my first fashion sketches.

At the time, my mother collected and bought patterns (*Vogue*, mostly) and would make her own clothes. We went to a fabric store, we took swatches of fabric—jerseys, gold lamé, and brocades—it was the beginning of me building a mood board. She would buy all kinds of rolls of fine wool and crepe, then she would make perfect dresses and suits. My sister and I were also the recipients of her talent: she made us charming dresses for special occasions.

Later in life, as a designer, when I had the opportunity to view an assortment of fabrics, I would get lost in the textiles. When they were presented to me at my studio, I would simply dive into the suitcase of the fabrics' representative to bathe in these beautiful, luxurious creations.

The mood board told the story, but more importantly, it allowed you to get lost and imagine that you were living in that era. But I also was entranced with the jewels, the cuffs, and the makeup. My father had always said, "Fotini, the Egyptians invented makeup."

Of course, I had to give a presentation—each child had to stand in front of the class and take the class through an explanation of the topic they'd been assigned. Typically I would be nervous, but something about my topic and the presentation just felt natural for me.

It felt more like someone had handed me a dream, and said to me, *You, Fotini, and fashion are the perfect fit.*

And so I began.

"The fashion of the Roman Empire owed a lot to the Greeks, but had a distinct style all its own," I said, voice steady, hand sweeping to my boards full of beautiful drawings and fabric swatches.

When you love what you do, it comes out naturally: and that was the day that I discovered that I loved talking about fashion. The kids clapped at the end of every presentation, but I remember the accolades I got for mine. I worked so hard, and I loved it so much. It was my first taste of something I'd come to discover the combination of not just loving something, but having it resonate with my audience. Getting an A+ from Ms. Teperkis felt like icing on the cake. But the grade was the lesser part of the reward. While I was working on the project, it didn't feel like a school assignment.

At another time, when I was eight, Tina had a particular Barbie I coveted. On yet another occasion while she was babysitting me, she broke the needle on my mother's sewing machine, which we had been warned to never touch. Tina proposed yet another deal: "Tell Mom it's your fault, and I'll give you that Barbie," she said.

I agreed.

Crying, I said, "I'm sorry, Mom, I accidentally broke the sewing machine." There was some yelling and more tears, and when it was done, I went to Tina for my reward. She was a glamorous blonde, in a pretty fuchsia mini dress and heels, bracelets on her arms. How I loved her.

"You're never getting that Barbie," Tina told me.

I did what any little sister would do in a similar situation: I went to my mother and sang like a canary! But the real justice was never done: I should have been given what wasn't given: Tina's Barbie.

The constant relocation continued. I was never used to it, but it felt more routine as time went on. When we moved to Regina, I was eleven. I claimed a space in the unfinished basement to play with my Barbies. I would disappear into my imaginary world. I would go down those basement steps, into the cool air, and enter a whole different world based solely in my imagination.

By the age of thirteen, in junior high, I was diagnosed with scoliosis, a curvature of the spine, which was pretty serious—hereditary from my grandfather. In those days the medical advice to cure scoliosis was to wear a back brace; I was in my teens and mortified. I was sure no one would like me: girls would make fun of me, no boys would be interested in me. I wore that back brace for two and a half years—for the last six of those months I'd hide the brace in my locker when I got to school and put it on before I went home. The brace had a metal circle around my neck and under my chin, two metal bars going down the back, one thick metal bar down the front attached to the circular neckpiece, and a cast-like plastic casing from my waist to the top of my thighs. *Unbearable.*

Even so, I had to sleep in this brace every day, and could only remove it for half an hour in the morning and half an hour at night to do exercises. I cried a lot. Sleeping and getting dressed with it on was especially hard. It was traumatizing for a thirteen-year-old girl to endure, and yet I did make friends (boys and girls) and ultimately, this contraption did mold my figure. By the time it came off permanently, it was as if my body was sculpted. That was the silver lining of the struggle.

As I grew older, I found solace in team sports, even though my father had expressly forbidden it.

"You're to come home and do your homework—getting good grades is more important than sports." My being around boys was also a concern for him. Even so, I managed to succeed through mild deception: when there were matches and meets, I just told my parents that I was staying at a friend's house. I enjoyed the competitiveness, and I believe it made me a better person.

As Tina and I got older, the five-year difference between us became more pronounced. Teenage Tina was beautiful, and I idolized her. I loved her clothes, and I was impressed by the bold personality that emerged when she hit her senior year in high school. I remember sitting in her room while she got ready to go out, watching her get dressed and put on her makeup. When her boyfriend pulled up on his Harley-Davidson to pick her up, she climbed on the back and rode away.

She is so cool, I thought.

After Tina left home, whenever she came to visit, the same thought always consumed me before she arrived: *What will she be wearing today?*

If she wasn't coming over to visit, I would go to her apartment to watch her get dressed for going out to nightclubs: how she'd blow-dry her hair and put on makeup. Sometimes I would even cook and clean for her. The truth was I got lost in watching her transform herself with clothes and makeup. We never looked alike: she took after the paternal side, and I took after the maternal side of the family. But one thing we shared that was identical was the shape of our eyes.

To complete her looks for nights on the town, Tina had to have the perfect clothes. There was a store in the mall called Suzy Cream-cheese, which was the *it* place to shop for cool going-out clothes. Black silk dresses, boas, even gold lamé jackets were the height of cool.

"Oh, I'm going to go to Suzy Creamcheese," Tina would say.

I'd say, "I'm going with you."

As I began to think about

In my heart of hearts, fashion had been what I wanted to do for a long time. But I had never voiced that, knowing it would be out of the question.

my own future, I was thinking more and more about fashion. The Barbies, the Roman Empire project, even Suzy Creamcheese—they held my attention and captivated my imagination. In my heart of hearts, fashion had been what I wanted to do for a long time. But I had never voiced that, knowing it would be out of the question. Finally, when I was a senior, I decided to just go for it.

"Fashion is what I want to do," I told my parents.

My father forbade it, saying, "Fotini, you have to understand business, and the most important industry is computers."

Reluctantly, I set out on the path my father insisted on. But like all the moves of my early life, the endless houses and schools, it was just another road leading me to who I really was. A designer.

CHAPTER FOUR

The Perfect Fit

It was like a fashion fairy tale.

—FOTINI

I stood in front of the Duomo, the *heart of Milano*, as the locals call it. It rose up, the marble façade intricately woven, the countless spires reaching to the steel blue Milan sky, each one punctuated by a statue or gargoyle. It was inspiring—enchanting, like a castle out of a storybook.

I walked along the cobblestone square—that square with gray pigeons rising up like clouds of silver ribbon in the wind, locals passing by hurriedly as tourists aimed heavy cameras at the spires—taking in the richness of the scene. And even though I'm not very religious, the Duomo brought a sense of solace. Being Greek Orthodox didn't stop me from saying a prayer and lighting a candle in a Catholic church—I don't feel that denominations separate us. I will walk into a Catholic church, a temple, and mosque for prayer. I may not go to church every Sunday, but prayer is part of every day for me. And so, even as the Duomo rose before me like a fairy-tale castle, I knew that there was not a princess, but prayer inside. I knew that I, too, was running on a dream and a prayer.

I had decided, in spite of the trajectory my father had set me on years ago, that I would return to my first love. After years of working with fashion and design from a business perspective, I was finally ready to make it the center of my life. Out came my pencils, my sketchbooks, my artistic eye. I had a portfolio of drawings back in my hotel room and appointments to make, but I couldn't resist the call of the city.

Aside from the Duomo, the place that called to me like a lilting aria was La Scala, the famed opera house where the great Maria Callas performed—a Greek woman of the fiery performances and undeniable chic.

Standing there, looking at her picture in front of the opera house on the cold, somewhat sterile streets of Milan, I couldn't help but think that Maria Callas could have been my customer. She was passionate, powerful, and had an enduring style that never faltered no matter her standing in the opera, in society, or even in love. When you see Dolce & Gabbana or Valentino send a cape-sleeved dress down the runway, or end their show with a wing-sleeved bride, you know they had Maria Callas in mind (at the very least, her arias playing softly in the background of their smoke-filled atelier).

Even though I didn't visit them, I walked by all the nightclubs, which were often tied to fashion houses—the Cavalli Club Milano, the Armani nightclub, and more. Aside from all this, the Duomo area was filled with a galleria of shops, chock-full of fascinating and vibrant inventory, especially compared to what was carried in North America. And beyond that, I found the famed street full of luxury designers, Via Montenapoleone, where studded jeans, jeweled pumps, and designs with opulence I'd rarely seen graced every window and shelf. I couldn't resist looking in shop after shop after shop, each like its own jewel box full of gems.

As the cold of the morning wore off into bright sunlight, I made my way to a place (not just a store, or a restaurant, but a whole city) called Peck, having skipped room service. Peck, established in 1833, is a gastronome's utopia of old-world Milan delights—inside you will find the most beautiful, wonderful, delicious food you can possibly imagine. I stepped down to the wine cellar, dark and gleaming and cool, thinking, *What is this place?* It was magic—the charm and history, the way the staff treated you like family—and it became my go-to stop for meals. After many long days scouting out ateliers and fabric mills, I would stop in at the historic

> *Because this wasn't all fairy tales and fantasy: this was hard work. Every fairy tale has a struggle.*

store and bring my meal back to my hotel. Because this wasn't all fairy tales and fantasy: this was hard work. Every fairy tale has a struggle.

The one true thing in common between this trip and all the others was that I was jet-lagged, tired, and exhausted, but I didn't care that the winter's damp cold shot straight through my bones—I was embracing it all. For the first time in a long time, it was my time, and I was going headlong into the experience. It wasn't a vacation: there was no time to relax. I plowed right through all the places I needed to visit, with an eye and mind toward my goal. All those years before, my father had encouraged me in another direction and I'd dutifully followed that path. And I'd been successful. It was partly what had happened in those years that brought me to that moment in Milan—to that pivotal instant in my life. Now I was on a mission toward my own dream.

My professional career began in computer programming, which naturally ricocheted to the marketing side of the business. Then I kept climbing the corporate ladder year after year: from sales and marketing to the financial industry; from the financial industry to corporate portfolio management; from corporate portfolio management to corporate and public affairs; from corporate and public affairs finally to store fixturing for luxury brands. That final position brought me in touch with something I'd not connected with in the corporate world before: luxury brands, fashion, and design. I'd unconsciously come full circle, until there I was with my dream right in front of me.

In all the years working in the corporate world, I had not dwelled on the dream I left behind, but coming into contact with those luxury brands stirred up an undeniable feeling. All those years of wanting to get into the fashion industry had been slowly simmering, and had finally come to a boil.

By that time (in my early forties) I had met the goals I set for myself in the corporate world, had two adult children from my first marriage, and had remarried a wonderful man. Still, when I left the corporate world behind, taking some time off, I wasn't feeling fulfilled by a life of social engagements and charity events alone. I was ambitious and had expectations of myself to accomplish and reach my potential, to use my expertise for my own ventures. That was when I decided not just to follow my path, but also to go into the industry that had been my first love: fashion. Now was the moment to figure out where my fit in that world would be.

I'd started to sketch again, but now this was no passing dream. Being an accomplished businessperson, I wasn't going to hop in blindly with starry eyes and unstructured dreams. I wanted to prepare and do it right. So I began my research immediately, exploring my options in Canada first. One of the Canadian fashion designers I reached out to seeking advice, Antonio Alves[1](and his partner), actually wanted me to run his business. They recognized my corporate background, saying, "Fotini, make us rich."

I thought about it for a moment. *Should I do it just for a little while?*

My next step was going to meet with a prominent female Canadian designer, Madeleine Boucher, who offered me the role of COO in her business. I politely declined. It was tempting, but in my mind I thought, *I'm not going to do this for anyone else anymore, it's time to do it for me.* I had always wanted to be liked; I had always tried to please. It was hard to say no to these tempting offers. It wasn't hard to say yes to my dream.

The silver lining that came out of these meetings was that one of the designers introduced me to Luca Matera, a fabric distributor out of Montreal. So off I went to Montreal, where my family had moved after Athens. As the plane landed, I thought, *This is where we first came to Canada.* It had always been a place of new beginnings for me, a bit of a contradiction because although it marked the start of my new adventure, it also felt like going home again. I met with Luca—a fireball Italian, a slighter version of Sean Penn—several times, brainstorming on how this dream could get up and running. I brought Luca my sketches and designs of the corsets I planned to produce. Corsetry was my true love. He looked through them one by one, with a discerning eye.

"If you really want to understand corsetry, we have to go to Italy." So that was what we did, and what led me to the Duomo in Milan.

We would visit fabric mills and old-world ateliers, and there I would (over the course of three years) study and work with the finest artisans in the fashion business. From Milan to Bologna and several

---

1   Throughout this book, many names have been changed to protect privacy.

stops along the way, this would be my proving ground. Italy was where I needed to go to figure out my plan. I would be let inside a secret world I had only dreamed about—never seen. I was on a mission toward my own dream, and nothing could stop me.

Luca—and his counterpart from Florence, Alessandro Ricci—were distributors and representatives of these magnificent, luxurious fabrics in North America. The two had working relationships with fabric mills and ateliers all across Italy. It seemed like a match made in corset heaven.

It was the quality of the sketches, our conversations about fabrics and silhouettes, which had made him suggest we go to Italy. There was something about corsetry I couldn't resist: the relentless attention to detail, the beauty of the female form, the way the corset itself trained the body into a beautiful shape.

Fotini, remember to wear your brace ...

But I wanted to design and produce corsets built into exquisite, luxury garments that would accentuate everything about a woman that a woman is meant to be in the most sophisticated way possible. That was something only done by artisans.

And so here I was in Milan, about to traipse through the places that just might be able to partner with me in making that happen. Along the way we would visit the fabric mills and jewelry makers, print shops and ateliers. Searching for the right suppliers to work with—those who would understand my aesthetic—was at times a challenge. I needed to feel it was the right fit.

But, as I stood there amidst the dizzying colors bursting from the shops in the Duomo, it was all just beginning. Our first stop was a trade show for all the fabric mills—where a whole industry comes to one place at one time. As are so many trade shows in any field, Milano Unica was endless and exhausting. But we saw a lot and learned a lot.

Over the following three years, from Milan to Bologna, from Como to Florence, we would jump through any hoops necessary to gain access to some of the world's most storied, old-world ateliers. But the hoops were worth it: I'll never forget Bologna.

There, in a town square with a lovely piazza was an exquisite fountain rising up from the cobblestone square, a carved angel springing with water that caught the soft Italian daylight as it fell. Luca, Alessandro, and I crossed the square and went up a first flight of stairs over a pizzeria on the first floor into the building. Then, once entering, we went up a second set of—winding, beautiful—stairs.

The staircase held an air of its history and the histories of those who traversed it, the pizzeria downstairs wafting terribly delicious scents as we passed. There were exquisite banisters leading up to a wooden door and when we arrived, we knocked—it was very old school. A refined gentleman (in his late sixties) and his wife welcomed us, speaking of course to Luca and Alessandro. There was a big painting of the original patriarch of the family—his face looked down on us with a keen eye as we entered. A superb crystal bowl, looking like it had been in the family for generations, was filled with fine chocolates. There was nothing ordinary about the place: you could see there was great respect and pride in every detail. To be in an Italian atelier is to be among the best of the best.

We stood in the corridor and I saw the wife ponder for a moment, then they took us to a meeting room. I didn't understand the language, but I was able to understand their body language as if they were saying to us, *You're fortunate to be here.*

We all sat down at an old wooden table, in a small room with a window where the afternoon sun filtered into the room: the top part of the window was clear, but the lower part was frosted for privacy. There was an air of elegance, of refinement. One wall was lined with

31

books, books I imagined held the archives of everything ever created here: every stitch and embroidery, every laced corset and jeweled bodice. I had my own sketches, a culmination of everything I loved: all the beauty of my childhood, all the elegance of women I admired, all the care and creativity I'd practiced so many years ago on those rainy days on the veranda in Toronto. This was the moment where the fairy tale came to life.

We took out the sketches and some of the samples of the fabrics. We were ready, showcasing not just the sketches, but also everything from the grosgrain ribbon that would be the back lacing of the corset, to the Swarovski crystals that would accent the closure. It was time to show them that I was deserving of being there and understood the world of luxury. They were working with some of the most elite brands in fashion, including Roberto Cavalli, Giorgio Armani, and Giambattista Valli. And then it happened: they took notice of my sketches.

I didn't have to speak Italian to know their reaction. I understood everything: from the body language in the room and the approval in their eyes. Suddenly, perfect espresso and fragrant biscotti—made by the wife—arrived. The hospitality, when they realized I was serious, was unparalleled.

It was then they decided we were special enough to go to their workroom in the back. As we entered the workroom and saw the worn but lovely faces of these artisans, every wrinkle, every worry line told a story as well. In the back room, scrumptious velvet was draped over a dress form, and the little ladies were looking at us with incredulous expressions. They didn't like us invading their territory! But they were such professionals and perfectionists: it's not just a job for them—it's a calling. *It's their art.*

And despite their high level of skill, they also had their little containers of food, and their messes here and there. All of it was a kind of contained discipline of madness that resulted in one thing only: luxury fashion. Those women were adept and accomplished artisans with a lifetime of experience.

Of course, what I noticed immediately were the corsets: velvet and silk corsets, made for Armani and Roberto Cavalli. This was what I aspired to be. And then I noticed the dress: grand, green, exquisite.

There it was, in the far back corner of the room, an unmistakable masterpiece of a gown, and just as I turned to view it, what should catch my eye, but two small women emerging from under the skirt just like the mice creating Cinderella's dress. They were tiny, their mouths full of pins, circling around the dress with every bit of magic as in Disney's classic.[2] I couldn't believe my eyes.

It was if I'd stepped into a fairy tale, and I knew that this dress was being constructed for someone important. The gown itself was an impossibly dark, mossy green taffeta. The top was a black velvet corset, off the shoulder with pleated green, capped taffeta sleeves, and a banner in green coming across the front over the black. The taffeta skirt came as an A-line from the cinched waist, then opened up into beautiful folds in the back, punctuated by a black velvet bow, and then another black velvet bow, and another.

It was like an imperial gown. It was then I asked who the gown was for.

The owner smiled, and said, "Queen Raina of Jordan."

Literally, made for a queen. But it was not the only grand dress there: there was another gown in the back and I asked whom that one was being made for. I was not going to get an answer for that one!

This is the truth of the matter: when you have a consistent elite client, as they did, you have a dress form made to their measure-

---

2   Clyde Geronimi, Hamilton Luske, and Wilfred Jackson, *Cinderella*, 1950, Burbank, CA: Walt Disney Productions, 1950, film.

ments. As I realized the refined creations in the room likely were for people of esteem all over the world, the dress forms took on a special magic. With one twirl of the artisan's wand, the magic became reality.

"We will give you an estimate on building the prototypes," the owner told us, snapping me out of the magic and into reality.

And so it was time to go eat some of the pizza we'd smelled wafting below us. We had been long enough with the scent; it was time to eat. What I'd seen floated through my mind, and I imagined those practiced, magical hands of the artisans making my sketches come to life.

Forty-eight hours later, they came back with a pricing quote per prototype. To build one prototype was an exorbitant amount of money. I had seven prototypes that I wanted. Each prototype would need to get reworked. I understood, but I said, "I can't do it." They were used to working with large, luxury fashion houses, but I was a start-up.

They were beyond capable, but they also were seeing me as an opportunity. This was a theme I'd come up against everywhere we'd been—the button suppliers, the print factories, etc.—so much so Italians who'd been in the business for decades saw me as a newcomer and, thus, as an "opportunity." The power balance was way off. When it's Roberto Cavalli or someone similar—there is an equal balance of power. I was new: the only true power I had was my business acumen, my ability to say no, to believe I could find a better way, and to keep opening doors

The perfect fit isn't always easy to find: perseverance is the key.

until I found the perfect fit. The perfect fit isn't always easy to find: perseverance is the key.

The search would continue as we headed to one of the best printing houses in the world, Ratti S.p.A., in Lake Como. On the way, we stopped for lunch at Harry's Bar, the legendary spot right in the main square of Cernobbio, with a breathtaking view of the lake and surrounding mountains from its elegant terrazzo. The minute we were seated I noticed a woman: chic, obviously a regular. And out of her Birkin appeared this little white dog, obviously more pampered than its owner, because the waitstaff immediately produced a bowl for the dog. "This is so great!" I said, smiling with Alessandro and Luca. It wasn't the celebrity or prestige that charmed me; it was the obvious hospitality and care toward their customer that caught my eye.

Ratti was a place apart. The prints hung on great racks, the way Persian rugs are hung from a ceiling, fanning out, each one more and more unbelievably striking in design. When I walked in to their facility I was like a kid in a candy store, lost in my own world. There were gorgeous samples of thousands of prints hanging in their archives with the highest level of couture prints I had ever encountered. I knew immediately that I would later want to develop my prints in partnership with Ratti. There's only one word to describe Ratti: legendary.

But we weren't finished. Onward to visit more manufacturers/ production houses in Chiari and Lombardy, which made bridal gowns and lingerie for some of the finest brands in the business. They were big operations: not something you turn down lightly. Business in Italy always includes lunch, where you talk about three things: family and politics, and then business. It was like a dream, this leisurely life in a tiny pocket restaurant in the town square. You have your wine; you have your espresso. It was unusual to me. In North America we don't practice this ritual regularly. It was this glorious existence and seeming ease, but the reality was that it was dead serious, and partnering with them would change the course of my life and work, forever.

When we returned after lunch to view their samples, some were gorgeous and some were clichéd gowns, almost peach cream puffs come to life—definitely not my style. They wanted me to develop my corsets there, inviting me to partner with them and become part of their design team. They were very serious and were putting a proposal together. Some fairy tales are not the right fit.

And once again, I knew that I didn't want to be partnering with someone else. I wanted to work on my own brand, FOTINI. It was ironic that everywhere we went I was seen sometimes as an opportunity, and other times as a means to boost their already existing brands. I knew that partnering with any of them would have been an easier way in, but I wasn't interested in taking the easy road. Anything worth having is worth fighting for.

And so on one of our last trips, we went to Alessandro's offices. He lived in a quaint little town just twenty minutes outside of Florence, but the offices were in the city. I stayed in the main piazza at a hotel he recommended, where he knew the manager. It was the dead of winter. It seemed I was always in Italy when the sky was slate gray and the air was bone-chilling cold. My exhaustion was also bone-deep—a jet lag born of so much travel and so many locations, all toward the same goal. And yet, it was beautiful. Snowflakes turned like icy jewels above the frozen river outside my window.

It was all very romantic, until I was snowed in on the day of my departure to Toronto. Due to extreme weather conditions, there was no way out and the airline didn't know when I could leave. I called my husband and broke down crying, asking if there was any way to get me out of there. Because one can be in the most beautiful parts of world, but the circumstances dictate your response to the experience.

Like the snow keeping me stranded, I realized that I felt stranded professionally in Italy. *Is it realistic to work here?* I wondered, as the unforgiving snow piled up. I thought of all I'd have to sacrifice to be based in Italy.

My time and life with my family. The complications of the language barrier. The challenging currency exchange.

I realized in that moment two things. One, that those were sacrifices that I was not willing to undertake. Two, that even though it was going to happen, it wasn't going to happen here.

This story was just beginning.

CHAPTER FIVE

Keep Moving

Every adventure requires a first step.
—LEWIS CARROLL, *ALICE IN WONDERLAND*

The towering elm trees created a canopy above me as I ran, my routine now every morning since I'd come to New York. I hadn't come here right away, or without any thought or preparation. I was methodical, a perfectionist.

Golden sun filtered through the leaves as my feet hit the cobbled pathway. One foot in front of the other in a rigorous run, but through the grand heart of the city where I felt the safest with my thoughts and emotions: Central Park.

Central Park became a safe haven for me, where I went to decompress, to find solace. And, yes, all the beauty and activity meant I could block out the noise of the city and in my mind. Wherever I ended up—in my eventual apartment and eventual studio, I knew I wanted—no, *needed* close access to the park.

My heart was beating double time to my pace, the heat on my face and the inevitable sweat of the hard work a result of my speed.

But my beating heart was also an echo to the questions in my mind, keeping up with scurrying thoughts of what I had accomplished to get this far. Skateboarders and roller skaters whizzed by as I moved past the stately statues, reminding me of all that had happened between Italy and now.

Upon returning to Toronto from Italy, I had tried to find production houses and seamstresses that could support my aesthetic and brand. I eventually came to the conclusion that, after exercising all of my options, it was not realistic to move ahead. I knew what I wanted my brand to be, but months of working with a top branding firm had secured my vision. It took extensive research about the marketplace to determine who my target market was: The FOTINI woman.

The park was a vision in itself and there were so many spots I felt compelled to visit on my runs: the Imagine Medallion in memory of John Lennon, with tourists flocking to pay homage; the gorgeous Bow Bridge with its fabled arch; and the peaceful boats in the pond with the famed Boathouse Restaurant behind them.

Other favorites of mine were The Mall and the Literary Walk (nicknamed the Promenade) that runs in the middle of the park from 66th to 72nd Streets—those beautiful elm trees.

At the pond, a small boy placed a boat on the silvery, dappled water and, even though he had the controller in his hand, the boat careened out of his reach, floating farther and farther away.

Birds sang and street performers danced for adoring tourists with cameras slung around their necks.

This is the pinnacle of the fashion world. I'm the new kid on the block, the unknown. It was exciting. I was afraid.

I continued on toward Bethesda Terrace, so beautifully constructed. My feet kept rhythm on the path and I recalled all the time I'd spent preparing for this moment in time. I hadn't come to New

York with a starry-eyed, pixie-dust, rose-colored-glasses enthusiasm. I came with a brand identity. A strategy. A plan.

Upon my return from Italy, I had worked in Toronto with the famed Bruce Mau Design team, and figured out my brand strategy. At first, I resisted naming the brand FOTINI. But eventually I came around to it.

Fotini means light—epiphany—it is who you are.

I kept running. Passing my favorite spots in the park felt like home. I reassured myself of everything I brought with me to New York. The FOTINI logo. The FOTINI hang tag. The FOTINI stationery. I had also brought along something essential: the initial vision of my debut collection.

As I exited the park, my thoughts went back to the statue of Alice in Wonderland.[3]

Have I fallen down the fashion rabbit hole?

I was jolted back to reality as I approached my hotel, where I would take a deep breath, shower, clean up, and tackle the day—off to the office.

I went to meet with David Randall of David Randall Associates before I moved to New York. DRA is a New York–based consulting firm specializing in retail and fashion. With an impressive clientele from the luxury sector, they became my advisors.

David Randall was impressed by the strategic and thoughtful way I approached my business, my distinct point of view, and how well versed I was on studying brands. This, coupled with my business experience, was the key reason he wanted to work with me. He knew that it is not enough to be creative in today's fashion landscape, but you must be a businessperson as well. He saw the right mix in me (preparation, vision, pragmatism) and in the FOTINI brand. I was serious.

---

3   Lewis Carroll, *Alice in Wonderland* (London, England: MacMillan, 1865).

David had been at Bergdorf Goodman previously and he had maintained his network there. After seeing my vision for the brand and the positioning of who the FOTINI woman was, he referred to Bergdorf, breezily stating at one of our initial meetings that his connections there would get the FOTINI brand in.

Teamed up with David Randall Associates, I began putting together the pieces of building the business, of bringing FOTINI to life.

And so the first collection begins—Spring/Summer 2012. One of my inspirations for the collection was my muse, Penelope Cruz, and her character from the movie *Blow*.[4] She was extraordinary. She represented dark beauty in a corrupt world, and that role was how I first discovered this Spanish actress—through her character Mirtha Jung. She was beautiful in an exotic way, mysterious—a seductress. The mood for this collection felt ethereal, echoing the mystery and femininity of a woman. Not sugary and girly, but sexy, confident, and chic—that was the vision.

The mood boards soon sprung to life, eventually becoming a wall: one after another.

My first collection in New York fulfilled a lifelong dream. Fashion dreams, after all, are what the clothes women love most are made of. Most respond to those that unabashedly embrace femininity.

So I began with a small wardrobe of the clothes I loved the most, clothes I dreamed of wearing, but could not find. It began with the simplicity of a stark white jersey blouse and a sleek black cigarette pant. Skirt suits—in banana yarn, or cotton kishi—are subtle in color and figure flattering, appliquéd with lace, or accented with an ivory faille corset and grosgrain ribbon lacing the back. Cocktail dresses are a favorite of mine—the first was a black-and-oyster Chantilly lace

---

4   Ted Demme, dir., *Blow*, 2001 (NYC, NY; New Line Cinema, 2001). DVD.

cinched at the waist. For a different mood was the strapless dress with a blush pink silk taffeta underlay and silk black tulle overlay accented with Swarovski crystals. These were but a few of the treasures in the collection.

From the vision in my head to a mood board and then to a sketch. And then—reality. The dream I first had in Como, Italy (where my love affair with Ratti S.p.A. and the hope to work with the legendary print house began) finally came to fruition. After meeting with the Ratti New York office, the collaboration began.

My first custom FOTINI print, the Javiera, had combined two images: blossoms and stems sourced from Spain, to create a slightly abstract floral pattern. There was a dark, black hole feel to one of the blossoms. It was eight to twelve colors, but it was imperative that the artwork should be developed so that one base color can be predominant over the others. It should read as a colored fabric with multi-color accents rather than a multi-colored print. The print should be elegant, sensual, and have a touch dramatic, while maintaining the youthful energy of the inspiration images, not overly intense or kitschy.

The process went back and forth between New York and Italy, where the prints were developed. Revisions were made until the perfect Javiera print was created. Ultimately, we would use it for the Simone, the Alexis, and the Calli dresses in the collection. There was a demand for the print, which was later made into scarves. The print fabric was ordered in a silk stretch satin and a silk georgette. This process proved to be one of my favorites—all the creative juices flowed into something customized and personal. But fashion isn't just about dreams, and clothes aren't made by magic.

Building the brand and a business meant building a team, too. I'd been living in a hotel for six months, and working in David Randall's office for that time, interviewing and adding people to my team: the team that would help me launch my first collection in New York.

We'd come to David Randall by way of LS Group. My husband and I met with LS Group, who had been recommended to us by the advertising and marketing holding company he worked with in New York. LS Group, a leader in the public relations arena, worked with well-respected and well-established design houses such as Ralph Lauren, Oscar de la Renta, and Diane von Furstenberg, DVF, to name a few. They were excited to work on this FOTINI brand.

After convincing us that their services would be right for FOTINI, we mutually agreed to work with them, as well as the retail strategist/consultant David Randall, who was introduced to us by Susan Costa, one of the cofounders of LS Group. There were meetings with Susan several times before anyone else in New York. I used David's office as studio space, as I searched for my own studio and a place to live.

I was staying in a hotel near the DRA office. There were nights I was so tired that I felt like I might have to crawl to what was then home. It was my runs in the park that kept me sane and made me feel like I could do this.

Anything you do in life that is not authentic to one's self is going to fail.

Interestingly enough, in my experience, whether meeting new collaborators, or building this business, you were expected to be "New York."

What does that mean? I found this odd. I thought you should be yourself, dress for yourself—for you and you alone. Anything you do in life that is not authentic to one's self is going to fail.

Be yourself, everyone else is already taken.

I wanted to find people for my team who abided by Oscar Wilde's adage, too. Finding the right people took time and some trial and error. In fact, when asked what is the hardest part about starting a business in New York, I always answer, "Finding the right people." That is true in any business, in any part of the world. However, we found the right people for that time, and one in particular stayed and played an important role for a long time.

First I had to find a production lead, the person who would oversee the budget, negotiate with vendors, and ensure quality control. They would act as the liaison between the design team and all suppliers for production, including the pattern makers and fabric manufacturers. My initial production lead, Barbara Marino, came to me from Carolina Herrera, where she led the production team there for several years. After the new technology was implemented at the design house and a new creative director took over the vision of the brand, her job became daunting and uninteresting to her; with FOTINI she found the old world of elegance and attention to crafts-manship that she loved and had a passion for. She was full of spunk and had that Italian charm; she was talented and took on a bit of a mother role toward me. It was a good match, and Barbara would become a staple of the team through several collections.

Jacques Rossi, the famed Frenchman who had talent and allure that only the French do, was one of the first New York ateliers I worked with. I used his pattern house/atelier for my intricate and detailed gowns and cocktail dresses: the draping and lace craftsman-ship were his favorite.

The first time we met was at his studio in a different part of town, where there were five long flights of uneven, wooden stairs to get to his front door. The stairwell smelled of stale smoke, but inside the atelier the smell vanished. Jacques was colorful, brilliant, and reluctant. He worked with some of the top design houses in the business. It was not an easy task to have him agree to meet with me, but when I took him through the designs, he was hooked. I gained the respect of one of the best in the business—not to be taken lightly.

Jacques would become essential on several collections in the FOTINI brand. Other members of the team proved tricky as well. There was Darren Lew, the technical designer who resented working for anyone but himself, but did it for financial reasons. He had lost his investment after running out of funds, a not-uncommon scenario for designers. He was also high a lot of the time and wouldn't be fully present until midday.

My first assistant, Dahlia, was most helpful—full of enthusiasm about being part of and growing a luxury brand. This was all a good start—unfortunately, eventually she felt working from the bottom of the ladder was beneath her. She craved more and more creative input, which she was not capable of. Dahlia came from a wealthy family in London—she didn't have the pressure of having to work. We would have to rely on her spark alone. I didn't need partners; I needed hard work and loyalty.

Andrea Lewis, whom David Randall had recommended I hire on as a marketing and sales VP, was also not performing. Her main role was to open retail doors for the brand and at the very least make introductions. She did bring some people on board—Barbara Marino, Jacques Rossi, and several others, but we saw nothing of the vast network she supposedly had. She was being compensated very well, but nothing came to fruition in opening retail doors, something of vital importance to a new designer. I was learning yet again about whom I surrounded myself with.

This lesson seemed to be a repetitive one.

I let Andrea Lewis go before the completion of the first collection. We were approaching New York Fashion Week, with buying season to follow, and I was in dire need of a sales representative.

One of the FOTINI team members from DRA went through her network of contacts and found Lisa Puglia, a spunky Italian woman in her early thirties with a hungry look in her eye. After my husband, a member of the DRA team, and I interviewed her (seeing that she had experience in sales and worked with companies like Escada), we decided there were not many other options and she did have those "hustle, shark like" qualities that could prove to be advantageous. We agreed to roll the dice, although I knew in my heart of hearts she was not the right fit for FOTINI—a little too rough around the edges. It was time to pray to the fashion gods, *please let this one work out.*

As we came closer to my first show, I finally found an apartment on the Upper West Side. I continued to put together the collection, working with seamstresses and all the other suppliers and artisans needed to create my designs. The Garment District is where fashion is born, where the ideas, visions, and creative come to life. Some designers run away from the area because of its lack of glamour, because of the gritty vibe (and smell). But the Garment District is where the suppliers are, with exception of a few like Jacques Rossi.

When I moved to my apartment on 57th Street between 8th and 9th Avenues, I figured it would be an easy twenty blocks walk down to the Garment District. I loved those twenty blocks.

At 8:00 a.m., cabs were whizzing by, past the street vendors lining the street and storefronts opening for the day. Schoolchildren rushed in groups to catch buses and Wall Street girls descend down subway stairs. I loved being in the thick of it all as I got closer and closer to where it all happened: the storied Garment District. American design houses I most admired still kept their studios there—Carolina Herrera and Oscar de le Renta, just to name a couple.

Exactly twenty blocks away from my apartment was an immaculately managed building, fifteen floors, filled with serious fashion clients from Cushnie et Ochs to Alexandre Birman, from Haute Hippie to the famed Betsey Johnson. With a red brick façade, it checked all the boxes for the kind of studio I desired.

On yet another whirlwind morning, with the wind on my back and sun warmly caressing my face, I began my day. Arriving at my destination, I pushed the elevator button to the fourteenth floor, and watched each floor number light up as I rose. Exiting the elevator to the right, I walked to the door and, with pride and tears in my eyes, turned the key in the keyhole and opened the door to my studio: 336 West 37th Street between 8th and 9th Avenues, Suite 1450.

It's really happening.

CHAPTER SIX

Hell Or High Water

When I dare to be powerful, to use my strength
in the service of my vision, then it becomes
less and less important whether I am afraid.

—AUDRE LORDE

That elevator ride up to suite 1450 became my morning ritual and—because 336 West 37th Street was part of the heart of the Garment District—more often than not, I wasn't alone. There were many colorful characters on the elevator with me, but there was one I always hoped to run into. He was around five feet nine with a slim build and sharp features, always on trend, chic, well-shorn, beach blonde fashion assistant, a poster boy for Malibu.

"You are on point today with that sequined dress," he said. "Especially in the rain."

"Oh, thank you, Ryan," I said. I was wearing one of my favorites, a little black-and-white racer back number. "You always look sharp and effortless."

He was in his early thirties, exceptionally polite, wearing skinny jeans in some bright hue, perfect sneakers, and always a great, crisp shirt that never felt stuffy. When my oldest daughter Georgia came to visit me from Toronto, he immediately invited her in to visit at his boss's studio. When she saw the labels strewn across the studio floor and all the prom-like cocktail dresses that resembled an assortment of colorful cupcakes, I thought she would pass out. But that's who he was: he could have been a diva, but he was very kind to everyone he met. Including me. Unfortunately, his friendly demeanor did not carry through to all of the other occupants in that building: that it did to me meant something.

Next door to the studio where he worked, I'd finally set up my own studio. It was everything I wanted it to be. Chic loft style—simple yet luxe. Old world yet modern. Fashionable yet elegant.

It was, in a word: FOTINI.

Originally the interior had looked like a box, with worn hardwood floors that had been recently refinished. But I knew how to make it warm, and with a fashion designer's flair. The main entrance door to the studio had a plexiglass square-cut sign that read: FOTINI. The sign was white with the word FOTINI in my signature logo—the elegant, custom silver lettering that was developed for the brand. It was surreal.

Not every day, but on certain days I would look at that sign before I entered the studio and I would get butterflies in my stomach. A range of feelings would hit me. It was emotional every time I looked at it, the worries of if I would make it, and for how long, echoing in my mind. *How long will this last?*

But I was determined to make it. And I'd created a beautiful studio to make it happen. When you entered, to the far left was a wall of windows, the center of which held two exquisite French doors that opened to a long, lovely balcony. On the far right the view was of the Hudson River, not to mention the rest of my fashion colleagues working away in the neighboring buildings.

Doesn't get better than that. I was in the thick of it now. Exactly where I wanted to be.

At the front entrance on the right there was a modern demi lune table with a mirror above it. As you walked further in, there was a white leather couch and organic wood coffee tables, which sat on a faux pony hair carpet. One of my pride-and-joy pieces was from a friend (who helped me set up the studio); it was an architectural rendering of the Chrysler Building, which we leaned against the wall beside the couch. And, finally, above the couch, going from one end of it to the other, hung a beautiful photograph of a rainy Central Park. If I couldn't be running in it or strolling its promenades, I could gaze at it there above the couch as I brought my collections to life. I needed Central Park with me everywhere: it was somehow my home, my true north in this new place.

I also included a rectangular glass boardroom-type table at which my team and I would collaborate—I always sat in the middle seat against the wall so I could touch my mood boards behind me and write on the white board. My assistant sat at the head of the table. Behind her, toward the window, were bust forms with draped fabrics, and sewing tables. At an antique teak table in front of the balcony doors sat my technical designer, working his magic. To the left of him were stationary shelves and cabinets. Then of course I had a kitchen area with all the usual accoutrements, with the inclusion of some fine china. Often there were cookies, chocolates, and other goodies in case we needed an afternoon sugar pick-me-up. The walls were filled with mood boards, photos that inspired me, sketches of each piece in the collection I was working on at the time. I also treasured beautiful fashion books: Alexander McQueen's *Savage Beauty*, Dita

Von Teese's *Fetish Goddess: Dita*, and Johnston, Kite, and Persson's *Nineteenth-Century Fashion in Detail*, to name just a few. Oh, how I adore fashion books!

As the crowning jewel, I'd brought and hung a French antique wrought iron chandelier from Toronto in the center of the room. And as we worked to prepare the first collection, the studio came alive. Beautiful samples of the beading that was designed, floret appliqués, Chantilly laces were strewn here and there. It became a place where the things I had dreamed became real. Sometimes they came together so effortlessly, but most times they came together with much effort, and long hours. It is hard to imagine or explain the monumental effort it takes to produce a collection, and even though Spring 2012 was small by fashion standards, it was my first. It was my trial by fire. And I was determined to get it right. Like I said, I am meticulous. So, around seven o'clock one evening we had the door to the studio open. It was a humid, New York evening.

"Let's get some air in here," I said, absentmindedly fanning myself, next to all the exquisite fabrics from the collection that sat on the pattern table. We were working with the Javiera print specifically. I was draping it on one of the dress forms. We didn't hear her or notice her when she came in, we were so entrenched in the work.

"Yoo hoo, are you still here? Hi, there, how are you?" A voice came bounding into the studio, startling us.

"Yes, hi! How are you?"

I couldn't believe my eyes, although I knew she was my neighbor and knew of her and rode the elevator with her fabulous assistant most days—I had yet to meet the legend.

She went straight to our pattern table and looked at everything on it and said, "This is great stuff." Furthermore, she started asking questions. "What *is* this brand? What do you do? Who is the designer?"

Now, most designers get very private about what they do. I was honored to share my vision, introduce myself as the designer: I was honored more so to explain my brand and aesthetic to my neighbor. To the legendary Betsey Johnson.

I took her through it all, took her through my mood boards, through the print design, through the collection, everything. She had on her signature tights, tutu, and red lipstick. We couldn't have been further apart, aesthetically speaking, but she really seemed to appreciate my vision. And I of course had great respect for what she had accomplished and how she built a brand that was always identifiable.

"Do you want a scotch, seeing you're working late?" she asked.

I smiled. "If I do that, there will be zero work done!"

"Well, if you change your mind, I'll be right next door."

I thought: *This woman may just cartwheel in next time!*

As NYFW approached, we were putting the finishing touches on the collection. Being in the Garment District proved to be a wise decision, as I had access to the production houses, pattern makers, fabric suppliers, and seamstresses—all very crucial. When you are in a time crunch, which is often the case every season, you can just run over to your suppliers. A designer has to embrace that there will always be last-minute changes and hiccups—it's the name of the game.

Simultaneously the casting of the models was taking place—everything happens at once. The girls you pick provide the canvas for your collection. The day came that young women were lined up and down the hallway outside my studio, all the way out into the lobby of the fourteenth floor. Each girl we turned away I reassured by saying, "You are very beautiful. Not being chosen is about my aesthetic and inspiration for this show, not about you." There were many sad, disappointed, and sometimes angry young faces when they didn't get the job. But it was true—they were all beautiful. I have always been in the business of building dreams, not crushing them.

Throughout castings over the years, I was disturbed to find diet pill casings, and some whole pills, in the front hallway; the girls would leave them on the demi lune in the entryway so I wouldn't see them. During that first casting, one girl nearly fainted; I shouldn't have been surprised. From then on I made a point of having light food at castings: fruits and nuts, things I knew they would eat. Once I made the mistake of providing mini-sandwiches and the girls avoided them like poison.

But we kept working, day in, day out, and many, many nights. The beading was sewn, the lace was affixed. The print was created, each seam checked, each corset refined. Castings finalized. Press invited, details refined, gowns perfected.

And finally, the day came. My first NYFW presentation. It was like throwing a party and wondering if anyone would come. I kept wondering in the back of my mind, *Will all the confirmed attendees show up?*

We set up at the Gramercy Hotel penthouse. Geographically (and quite strategically) we were set up close to Marc Jacobs and Oscar de la Renta, among others who were presenting that day. It is wise to position yourself very purposefully around well-known designers, as editors, buyers, and the who's who of fashion will be most likely to stop by and see a new designer if they are positioned on their way from one big fish to another. If they had to cross town to see you—a new and an unknown designer—they probably would not cross town.

We did a presentation format instead of a runway. For one thing, it made it easier for editors, retailers, and guests to approach the models and examine the intricate details on the clothing. But the decision was also my business sense kicking in: runway was too ambitious for a start-up. The expense was far too much, and it would have come across as ostentatious—like I was trying to prove something as a new designer. You cannot avoid the critiques and judgments: you need to learn how to manage the ones that matter.

I intended to show my vision and communicate the aesthetic of the brand. That penthouse was everything that FOTINI the brand was: opulent, feminine, with a little dark, daring, and mysterious thrown in for good measure. It was sexy without being overt. Everything about that penthouse had an old-world richness that reflected the kind of staying power I hoped to build in the fashion industry. Because although I was the new kid on the fashion block; although a fashion guru in Toronto had once told me, *You're not a designer*; although some in New York had taken me less than seriously; although some had looked at me and thought, *You're not that young, a new protégé, or a recent graduate ... she'll never make it*—this collection, these clothes in this room on this day, September 12, 2011, before New York's fashion editors and elite, was my proving ground.

This room was a jewel box and these clothes were the kind of jewels you want to keep forever.

The first thing you would notice stepping into the room was the cool elegance of the deep blue walls, transporting us all to a kind of galaxy of chic. I don't remember feeling that level of glamour since I was a little girl, watching the dazzling Greek women circle the room in their jewels and dresses while my grandfather held sway over the room. But this was my creation. The room was decorated with gorgeous, rectangular floral arrangements of maroon-colored roses and crimson dahlias that perfectly set off the elegant, classic beauty of the models, the way they wore their femininity, draped as they were across the deep ruby velvet couches and sleek sapphire velvet divans.

All of it: the colors, the models, the flowers, and—of course— the collection—was a personification of FOTINI. The models changed their clothes throughout the evening, except for the two show-stopping gowns, the Isabella and the Gaga. From the Lola cocktail dress in the oyster and black Chantilly lace, to the flirtatious sequin Britney skirt, and chic jersey Elle blouse, the collection had something for every FOTINI woman. The Javiera print was shown in two ways—the elegant, corseted column-like Calli gown in stretch silk satin, and in the playful silk georgette Simone dress.

So full of feminine power and mystery, a hint of sexiness and danger and the undeniable alluring beauty of everything a woman is meant to be. The models were positioned—some on the couches, some sitting ladylike on the chaises, a few standing in their power—around the room as if you were entering an elegant cocktail party, a timeless affair. Their long hair tumbled loosely in gorgeous, sleek curls about their luminous, glowing faces. They wore towering, T-strap, peep toe sandals to show off long shimmering legs that peeked out of the exceptionally well-tailored Rebecca pant or the cascading tulle overlay of the impeccable and dramatic Gaga gown.

It was a deceptively quiet room, with sensual Buddha lounge music playing from hidden speakers, for an unquiet collection. The corsets—whether it be the stand-alone Victoria, or those built into the Calli or the Gabriella gowns—did not go unnoticed. And then, at the end, the two gowns appeared. The Isabella was a three-tone corseted, Grecian-style gown in beautiful earth tones. The Gaga— also corseted—had a blush pink taffeta base with black tulle overlay. The back of the dress had beautiful lacing in black grosgrain ribbon with an explosion of silk tulle hand placed in blush, black, and oyster to finish off the mermaid-like silhouette.

And all at once, I couldn't believe how quickly it went by. In an instant, it was over. Like a dream, like the fairy tale, that story was over. After NYFW, buying season begins. Buyers come in from large and small retailers, including specialty boutiques. For the next week, your sales representative has appointments booked ahead of time, with buyers who come to view the collection. They decide if they will pick you up. I had a couple of models reserved on the days that the important buyers came in—in my case they were all important, because no one had heard of FOTINI.

I would have the girls wearing signature pieces to begin with, but as the buyers went through the collection, they would request to see the pieces they were interested in on the models. That first season, I had my studio set up as a sales showroom.

We took out a lot of the furniture and made a quaint little showroom with the necessary items on hand: a seating area, a desk for writing orders—which every new designer prays for—and, of course, lovely china. The clothing racks had the treasures hanging from them ready and on display. Again, being cost-conscious, this made a lot more sense than being in a showroom, which would then take a percentage of any sales made. It worked out really well.

I had three racks of clothes and lovely refreshments—cheese and crackers, cookies and fruit, and my signature macarons. Everything was served on china and with silverware—no plastic plates. It was all tastefully done without going overboard. The buyers are exhausted, so it's important you make them feel comfortable and that they can unwind. It is a tiring job they have.

That season, three buyers from Bergdorf Goodman came in. One of them was particularly negative, with a kind of *You're so lucky I'm here* attitude. Her boss, Emma, on the other hand, was so gracious. The third really didn't say much at all. Of course I was very nervous. And of all days, when Bergdorf was coming, both my models didn't show up! The modeling agency had made a scheduling error and sent them across town. It was Bergdorf Goodman and they had made a mistake! I must say the two buyers were very gracious and understood, reassuring me that it was okay and that this happens.

The process is as follows—the buyers give you a critique based on their vision for their customer. But you cannot change for each store: financially speaking, it is impossible. You can make tweaks, for example: the standard hem of a dress or skirt can vary depending on the customer and demographic. You can change the fabric of a garment, while the pattern/silhouette stays the same. In a warm climate they may request it in a silk chiffon rather than a tweed, and in a four-season climate they will request accordingly either for Spring/Summer, or Autumn/Winter, or Resort and Pre Fall. Designers go broke trying to make changes according to the notes they get from buyers. It happens that stores will come back and say, "Sorry, we're not picking you up this season," after designers have made all the changes. More often than not a new designer does not get picked on their first season. Buyers want to see a proven sales record and consistency of a brand before they commit. This can take several seasons, which is frustrating to the designer as they struggle to stay in business.

The critiques are endless—you cannot be everything to everyone. As a new designer, it is important to listen and not be arrogant (a know-it-all), but there is a limit. When the compromising of your *designs* starts to compromise your *brand* and, further, financially it is not feasible? Don't do it. Make tweaks, but do not change your aesthetic. So when Bergdorf gave me notes, did I make all the changes they suggested? No. I made a few revisions here and there, but only if I thought it could help my brand, and only if I thought it would improve the collection from a sales standpoint.

Their recommendation to me was to stay in the cocktail/evening gown category. You see, they have an extensive selection at their store and perhaps that is what their budget allowed for, but, for me, I didn't want to be pigeonholed. I understood that my cocktail/evening was very special, but I wanted to dress a woman for all occasions. I continued with what I felt in my heart.

You have to prepare line sheets that explain the length of the skirt, the inseam of the pant, the American size versus the European size. This is where a seasoned, professional sales representative is key—and this proved to be my biggest challenge. Toward the end of the buying season week, on an early evening appointment, two women came in from the rain. They were tired and somewhat agitated from their full day of viewing other designers. I offered them water, coffee, or tea, and the one who was the store owner (and clearly in charge) said with a laugh and a sigh, "Do you have any red wine?"

I was happy to serve red, white, or champagne.

The store owner turned out to be Sara Peters, the owner of a Texas boutique, and her assistant. Sara was a former Southern beauty queen. She and I connected right away, and her second-in-command was professional and lovely. You know how they say, *when you know, you know*?

I knew. And sure enough, Sara started in right away when she became a little more comfortable. The truth is, she got excited when she went through the collection and saw some of the pieces on the models.

"These fabrics are exquisite. This is craftsmanship. They are all so special, Fotini," she told me. She signaled to her assistant to take pictures on her iPad. "This would be great for Miss Betty... This would be great for Daphne..."

Sara had specific customers in mind for specific pieces. It was so interesting to see her process of ordering for the boutique. As opposed to how a retailer like Saks would order—"We need seven sized ten, eight sized two"—Sara was like a personal shopper, friend,

59

and confidante to her customers.

The sales representative usually takes the buyers through the collection, explaining in fine detail the advantage to picking up this brand. While Lisa had brought in Sara's boutique, she was not very sophisticated and did not understand the brand as well as she should have. She had come in just before NYFW with little experience on what FOTINI represented. At one point Sara did say to Lisa, "Missy, you had better learn how to sell this brand—it is very special."

I then took over and sold it to Sara. No one else could talk to the brand like I could: my blood, sweat, and tears had gone into this. Then Sara and her assistant took out their order forms. I couldn't believe it—could this be my first order?

It was a moment of pure euphoria! But I also told myself, *Now is not the time for that dance of joy you usually break into in times of triumph.* I didn't know what to do with myself. FOTINI was officially in business!

> *I didn't know what to do with myself. FOTINI was officially in business!*

I went home that evening and did a dance of joy, poured myself a glass of Frog's Leap Sauvignon Blanc, and called my husband in sheer glee. I called my parents, and they were so proud and excited for me. Yet I couldn't help feeling alone and needing to hug someone. To my surprise, even in that celebratory moment, a rush of bittersweet emotions came pouring down my cheeks.

But fashion doesn't stop for anyone, and so the next morning I went right back into the studio and no sooner had I arrived when the phone rang. It was Helen Stone from LS Group, my PR firm, who had been in charge of the FOTINI presentation. A small terror ran through me at the sound of her voice, wondering if I'd received press for my first collection, or if I'd received no press at all. As a new designer, I was terrified of any bad press from a major fashion influencer.

"It's WWD," she said.

"Is it good?" I asked, with a numbness coursing through my entire body.

"It's more than good," she said.

Relief flooded through me as Helen read the quote aloud. This was the dream. It was the day after and we couldn't believe that WWD not only mentioned FOTINI, but had a positive quote.

"Inspired by strong and confident women, Fotini Copeland debuted her Fotini Collection in an intimate presentation with delicate lace dresses, ethereal Grecian gowns, flirty sequined skirts and sweet ruffled blouses, all with a romantic yet modern hand ... Congratulations, Fotini! Well done."

The FOTINI debut had been a success: wonderful turnout, press beyond what we had dared to dream, and—best of all—actual orders from the line.

But the memory that stays with me the most from that time is the night after my presentation in NYFW, when my family and close friends and some of the team—maybe twelve or fourteen of us— went for dinner to the downtown Cipriani (a favorite) to celebrate. Then a smaller group of us, immediate family and very close friends, went for a drink on a rooftop. New York rooftops, wasn't that another defining part of so many New York stories? As iconic as my runs through Central Park felt, there was the way the city lit up from the rooftop, the dark sky overhead, the skyline glimmering with all the windows lit up, almost as many it seemed as there were stars in the sky. We were sitting having cocktails at the Peninsula Hotel on a warm and sultry September evening, and I thought to myself, *Now you're becoming one with New York.*

I looked out on the city—with my closest beloveds from Toronto so excited and happy—and I remember thinking, *On to the next, the sun is going to come up.*

But at that moment I soaked it all up. I was with the people who loved and supported me under the glittering stars and lights of New York City. And the next day another day dawned, and even though it was a miserable, rainy, New York day, hot as could be, I put on a dress: it was a T-shirt dress made of crepe de chine, the piping on the neck and sleeves were black. The base of the dress was white and on top were colors of pink and caramel, it was like layer cake with an overlay of silver sequins. Like I said, it was hot and muggy, and oh, did I mention pouring rain? My loved ones had returned to Toronto and, even though this new life could be lonely, I said to myself, *I refuse to feel down, I'm going to put up my hair in a high pony, slip on those heels, and wear sequins.*

And I did. And I went to my studio. Angela, my social media manager, came in and said, "I can't believe this. I have to have a photo of this. I have to take a photo of this while you're sitting at your glass table working away."

So she ended up taking a photo of the bottom of the skirt and my high heels. That dress—the whole premise is if I feel I want to wear something beautiful, come rain or shine, I'm going to wear it. Rain be damned. It was the racer back dress—the one the fashion assistant had complimented me on in the elevator in the early days of building my first collection. And now I was creating my second.

You are your brand. And FOTINI, the designer and this brand, was here to stay.

Come hell or high water.

CHAPTER SEVEN
Legacy of Creation

There are never enough hours in the days of
a queen, and her nights have too many. .
—ELIZABETH TAYLOR AS CLEOPATRA,
FROM THE FILM *CLEOPATRA*[5] (1963)

I had expected entering the New York fashion world to be incredibly difficult, but I hadn't anticipated *what* would be difficult. I was learning how small the fashion community is, and where the decision-making power rests.

It turns out it's not a myth: if Anna endorses you, magic happens. A goal and dream for most designers. I was also learning the power of being, as some said, "that nice Canadian lady." Top-notch people were working with me, despite my limited resources and inexperience, for several reasons: they loved the designs/craftsmanship and were excited about making them come to life; I treated people with basic respect; and, perhaps most importantly, I paid on time.

---

5   Joseph L. Mankiewicz, dir., *Cleopatra*, 1963 (Century City, CA: Twentieth Century-Fox Film Corporation, 1963). Film.

A couple of months after NYFW, my advisors, strategists, and I came to the conclusion that LS Group, our PR firm, was not working out. We were paying their high monthly retainer, and we were not getting a return on our investment. As it turned out, the very thing that had been so attractive about the company—their impressive client list—was a problem. With so many heavy hitters taking priority, they spent almost no time or energy on the FOTINI brand. It was time for a change. We let LS Group go, and signed on with a medium-sized agency called Karen Baker Communications, who reassured us we would get their full attention.

I also began to learn that there would always be people working an angle. Lisa introduced me to her designer friend Gabriela Nowak (although at the time I didn't realize it was a setup). Gabriela, too, was a relatively new designer struggling to get her brand recognition, but she also needed financial backing. An evening out for drinks and dinner with Gabriela and her boyfriend turned into a hard sell to invest in their company, and after I declined, we met "by chance" twice more, and they repeated the performance. Between Gabriela's pushiness and Lisa's "borrowing" clothes from the collection without asking for her social outings, supposedly to represent the FOTINI brand, I decided to sever my relationship with Lisa, which turned messy. The whole thing left a bad taste in my mouth, but it was a reminder—be careful whom you bring into the fold.

It was surreal, like a dream. As I walked the twenty blocks from my studio to my apartment on many days, many thoughts stirred through my mind.

You gained the respect of the seamstresses—of your peers.

This thought was triggered because that afternoon I had to pop in to see one of my lead seamstresses at one of my pattern houses. I was greeted with respect and smiles. I was extremely proud of that, but I was only going into season two. I felt this was finally real.

Stay focused and disciplined, Fotini. Eyes on the prize.

In fashion, there is no resting on your laurels. You're only as good as your next collection. Before I was wrapping up the first show and making my first sales, the creative ideas and inspiration for my next collection were flowing. Typically, the process sees the designer already building the concept of the next collection while working on the production of the collection they've just shown during fashion week.

The next collection's inspiration was so organic: I wanted to pay homage to the two cultures that I came from, Egyptian and Greek. This second season was about to represent who I am—so I was ready to tell *my* story through this next collection. How important it was to find the most authentic way to tell the New York fashion world who I am. To that, I added the alluring and captivating magic of queens and goddesses, whom I had so admired growing up.

It was authentic, natural. My mind kept swirling with those queens and goddesses of my heritage.

CLEOPATRA

Regal Egyptian queen, raised to rule, immortalized
throughout history.

NEFERTITI

Exotic beauty beyond compare and wife of Ramses;
born outside royalty but rising nonetheless to legend.

APHRODITE

Greek goddess of love, symbol of femininity,
sensuality, passion.

ISIS

Magical healer of the sick, bringer of life, most maternal of
all Greek goddesses, powerful and exquisite.

These images lived not just in my mind, but also in my soul. Because this was my heritage, these were the tales my father and grandparents had told me, the stories I had pored over in my encyclopedias as a girl. This was recognition of what had shaped me. Born in Athens to a father who had been born in Egypt, I felt I was meant to create this collection.

As with all collections, my inspiration didn't come from a single source. Aside from queens and goddesses, I was inspired by a perfume bottle, a relic discovered in an ancient Egyptian queen's tomb, that I inherited. Another inspiration was the 2004 movie *Troy*, the ethereal gowns and gold-leaf crowns of a woman who was coveted and loved.[6] It was also Autumn/Winter and the fabrics are extremely rich. There were such beautiful fabrics that season and the custom print was gorgeous. I named the print I developed for that collection Ramses after Yul Brynner's character, the Egyptian king, in the movie *The Ten Commandments*.[7] I'd always been captivated by beauty in various forms, by defining moments in both film and life.

What if I could capture the mystery, the power, from this Dark Age, and juxtapose it with the modern, chic, feminine style of the FOTINI woman? I decided the silhouettes would have to be different this time—they needed to stand alone, more dramatic like their namesakes. It must be love at first sight. All women must thrill to these icons as I did.

---

6   Wolfgang Petersen, dir., *Troy*, 2004 (Burbank, CA: Warner Bros. Pictures, Inc., 2004). DVD.

7   Cecil B. DeMille, dir., *The Ten Commandments*, 1956 (Hollywood, CA: Paramount Pictures Corp., 1956). Film.

Yes, fashion is a business, but it must first be a true passion. And this upcoming collection blended everything dear to me. But in spite of my excitement and anxiety, I continued to work hard on production of the Javiera Collection, the overlap between collections being a fact of the fashion life.

Going into my second season, I began to make some changes both in my team and the outside people we worked with. I replaced my assistant, Dahlia, with Jennifer, whom I hired out of Ralph Lauren—Ralph Lauren being jokingly known in the industry as "the internship" because they worked the assistants hard while giving them an intense fashion training that was like gold on a résumé. Jennifer was spunky, sweet, and smart as a whip. I also needed a technical designer since Darren had been let go, and I found one in Gino Canali. Gino was not just wonderful at his job; we became fast friends, sometimes making each other laugh so hard we could barely breathe.

I wanted to work with a stylist with the same vision as I had, and who truly understood the brand's aesthetic. I had not felt that connection with the stylist from the first show, but I was not going to repeat that mistake or second-guess my intuition.

Christina Moretti, an employee of David Randall's who had become a good friend, told me jokingly, "I have a friend, Allison Hart, but I'm almost afraid to introduce you because you're kind of the same person. Allison's great at what she does. She travels with Oprah, and she works with *O Magazine*."

Could this be the perfect stylist for FOTINI?

I had been having trouble with stylists—everyone was coming in with their own rather forceful ideas of what they wanted FOTINI to be—which was usually too frilly, too edgy, or just too *not FOTINI*.

I then met Allison. And while Christina had been joking about being afraid to introduce us, I soon discovered she was right. It was uncanny how Allison and I had the same vision for the presentation and for fashion, not to mention the similarities in our personal lives.

Allison Hart: a soft-spoken, very pretty, petite, caramel blonde with an incredible work ethic and focus. She arrived, started viewing the collection, and began pulling shoes and accessories as she went along, as if she had sprung fully formed from my mind—it was truly seamless. She studied the clothing carefully, minutely detailing each item in a notebook and going over it all with me. Allison came prepared, and she was very impressive. It's not surprising that she became a dear friend.

I added a second production house to supplement Jacques Rossi, as this was a larger collection. I chose the talented, raven-haired Grace Tsui, whose pattern and production business was growing in popularity. She was so good that fashion houses were coming to her in droves, and I added her while hoping she wasn't in over her head.

Meanwhile, Jacques and I were about to go head-to-head.

The centerpiece of my collection was to be the Cleopatra gown: midnight black, made of laser-cut leather and feathers.

"This is *not* a good idea," Jacques said to me, resolute, the first time he saw the design. He didn't understand why I wouldn't just do it with fabric—he found leather for this particular gown rather "gauche." But my vision was a modern and chic twist on the classic mermaid silhouette. In the most professional manner, we argued. Now, Jacques Rossi had one of the most in-demand design and production houses in New York, working with a long list of top designers. He had strong opinions about how he wanted to work and what his vision was. But his vision was not mine. I always, always stay true to myself, and my vision for this dress was crystal clear. We went back and forth, back and forth, passionately arguing our points. At last, Jacques conceded and did what I had envisioned. When it was done,

Childhood and Family Photos

Fotini's father and mother,
George and Calliopi, on a date

Fotini's christening with
Godfather Ernesto

Father and Grandfather Kosta
in Athens

Grandmother Fotini, far left

Mother, sister, baby Fotini, and
Grandmother Katherine

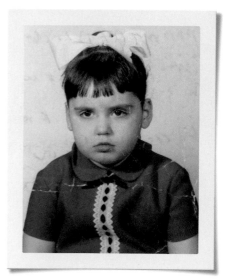

Passport pic for travel to Greece

Fotini in the red patent shoes in the front row, with teacher
Ms. Armstrong and classmates; first grade, Montreal

With favorite doll, Swingy, in Greece

High school graduation

SPRING 2012

The Javiera Collection

Inspired by Penelope Cruz and her character from the movie *Blow*:
sexy, confident, chic—and dangerous.

FOTINI

INVITES YOU FOR COCKTAILS
TO INTRODUCE

THE 2012 SPRING/SUMMER
COLLECTION

MONDAY, SEPTEMBER 12
6 UNTIL 8 IN THE EVENING

GRAMERCY PARK HOTEL
PENTHOUSE
2 LEXINGTON AVENUE
NEW YORK CITY

RSVP

Clockwise from top left: Spring/Summer 2012 invitation,
Penelope Cruz as Mirtha Jung in *Blow*

Clockwise from top left: Fotini with presentation models at the
Gramercy Park Penthouse; Georgia cocktail dress beading;
presentation models; opulent, yet moody florals at the presentation

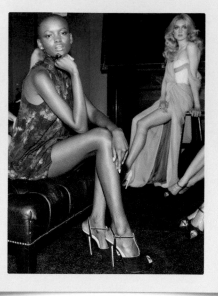

Clockwise from top left: Javiera custom print;
presentation models; ethereal, yet dark inspiration;
behind the scenes at the presentation

Clockwise from top left: presentation models;
mysterious inspiration; Gaga gown;
damaged yet beautiful inspiration

Egyptian Queens and Greek Goddesses Collection

Inspired by Egyptian and Greek goddesses:
Cleopatra, Helen of Troy, Queen Nefertiti

Clockwise from top left: Laser cut velum invitation;
presentation models at New York Fashion Week at Lincoln Center;
Ramses cocktail dress in custom print

Clockwise from top left:
Aphrodite gown with Zoe cape; Cleopatra inspiration;
Anastasia coat; Cleopatra gown

Clockwise from top left:
Isis gown; Isis sketch; Helen of Troy inspiration;
back of Cleopatra gown

Clockwise from top left: Nefertiti gown; Nefertiti gunmetal embroidery; Olympia cocktail dress; Fotini with Linda Fargo, Senior Vice President of Bergdorf Goodman, at the Lincoln Center Presentation

The Wisteria of France Collection

Inspired by the Provence region of France:
sunlight, flowers in bloom, the gentle caress of spring breezes.

Clockwise from top left: Fotini in Margot cocktail dress putting the finishing touches on the model before show time at Lincoln Center; Emmanuelle gown sketch; New York Fashion Week invitation featuring custom watercolor wisteria; Angelique dress with Madeline jacket at Houston Fashion Week

Clockwise from top left: Georgia cocktail dress at Houston Fashion Week;
Emmanuelle gown up close; Amorette cocktail dress;
Colette cocktail dress at the New York Fashion Week presentation at
Lincoln Center, featuring garden in Provence inspiration

Clockwise from top left: Veronique blouse with Jeannette short at Houston Fashion Week; Margot cocktail dress sketch; Emmanuelle gown at Houston Fashion Week; Camille suit

Clockwise from top left: Marie Antoinette gown at Houston
Fashion Week; behind the scenes featuring the Jacqueline dress;
Marie Antoinette gown sketch; Provence Inspiration

Georgia's Wedding Dress

Inspired by a fairytale princess marrying her prince.

Clockwise from top left: putting the finishing touches on the wedding day,
July 6, 2013; front of dress sketch; dress fitting with FOTINI team
at the New York studio; back of dress sketch

Amy Poehler
in the Cleopatra
gown at the
Met Gala, 2012

The Romanov Collection

Inspired by the opulence and intricacy of the Russian Romanov Era,
including Catherine the Great, Fabergé eggs, and amber gemstones.

FOTINI CORDIALLY INVITES YOU TO AN INTIMATE PREVIEW OF T

FALL 2013 COLLECTION

TUESDAY, MARCH 12TH, 2013
8:00AM - 5:00PM

THE PIERRE
2 EAST 61ST STREET BETWEEN MADISON AND FIFTH AVEN
SUITE #1714

BY APPOINTMENT ONLY

Clockwise from top left: Invitation for the private showing at
New York Fashion Week at the Pierre Hotel; Katerina gown;
embroidery inspiration; Lubov gown sketch

Clockwise from top left: Vasilisa dress featuring a Romanov custom print;
the Amber Room at Catherine Palace, Saint Petersburg, Russia;
Sofya dress; Nadine corset with Nika skirt

Clockwise from top left: Romanov custom print;
Ozera blouse with Rebekah pant sketch;
inspiration; Raina cocktail dress

Clockwise from top left: Natalia dress; Tanya corset with custom embroidery; Georgia gown sketch in second color way of custom print; Fotini with Adam Glassman, Creative Director of O, *Oprah Magazine* at the collection preview

Featured Press

Beloved Bronx the Yorkie

he loved it. I had picked the right battle.

The collection was coming together—using only the finest Italian fabrics, French lace, leather, and beading to create intricate finishes in deep, burnished shades, all built on the foundation of FOTINI corsetry. It's about the foundation and the fabrics, not just the designs. And this collection dared to be different, from the feathers to the laser cutting, the crinkled chiffon, the sleek charmeuse, the silk lame, the wool bouclé, the Ramses print from my beloved Italian print house Ratti. That print will always take me back to watching *The Ten Commandments*, the way you can practically see the shape of the Pharaoh's head, the visual magic as the rich, deep colors catch the light.

> *It's about the foundation and the fabrics, not just the designs.*

The mallard green silk Grecian gown paired with the gleaming iridescence of the green and bronze tip-feathered Zoe cape. The bronze silk Artemis cocktail dress with its snake-inspired chain neckpiece. The navy and charcoal wool lace Gardenia dress. The charcoal snakeskin jersey Nefertiti gown with detailed gunmetal embroidered snake on the back. And, of course, the corseted black laser-cut leather lace Cleopatra gown with its fulsomely feathered bottom.

These were just a few pieces from the Egyptian Queens and Greek Goddesses Collection that we were putting the finishing touches on right up until literally the last minute. The designs were challenging, particularly the Nefertiti, with the tricky placement of the snake on the back. It had to start at the shoulder, curl down the back, and end just below the waistline. I had to answer pattern questions such as "How do you want the snake? Curled? Curved?" And it had to be a design that could be made to fit more than one woman. Real women's shapes and sizes vary. The night before the show, I was equally excited and nervous. A show at Lincoln Center for New York Fashion Week! Not a suite at a hotel, but a strategic move to get more traffic. Not to mention a prestigious site famed for the arts. Lincoln Center. On stage. NYFW. This was happening for me, with just my second collection. It was a wonder I could think straight.

There were approximately fifteen people in the studio long past midnight. Two young men had rushed over from their last job to hand-sew the feathers on to the bottom of the Cleopatra gown, a delicate task. Unlike the Zoe cape, which featured stiff, structured feathers, I wanted the Cleopatra gown to have movement in its mermaid's tail, to flow. Yet the rest of the gown needed to be structured and remain just so on the body, not an easy feat with malleable, laser-cut leather. To get the desired effect, the leather had to be fused with a stiffer material—in this case, deep green taffeta—while the profusion of feathers had to be carefully chosen and sewn on by hand. Everyone was exhausted but pushing themselves to get across the finish line. Then I heard Barbara Marino say, "We'll never get this done in time. It will never work."

When she said those words, I saw the hand of one of the two young men shake as he stitched, and the mood in the room shifted ever so slightly.

"Get out—I don't want you here! I don't want you anywhere near the show," I told Barbara, anger heating my voice.

She apologized, but I still asked her to leave the studio for the night. I couldn't let one person's doubt and negativity bring down my whole team. We had all worked too long and too hard to let that happen. Not to mention, she was wrong: we did finish in time, and it did work. The next day she apologized again, and I let her come to the show—despite her comment the night before, she had worked hard on the collection and was proud to be a part of it because she had been the production lead. Still, it weighed on my mind that her negativity was beginning to sound like a broken record.

And so the day arrived—Tuesday, February 14, 2012—my second collection, my first at Lincoln Center. I had chosen a presentation format, for the same reason as before: my clothes were always about details, and the best details would be lost on a runway, with the models breezing by. This time they stood on platforms at different levels, the leather Cleopatra gown at the top.

Like the queens and goddesses who had inspired me, the models stood on their plinths, regal and iconic. I saw before me everything I had envisioned: the dramatic color palette, the exotic details, the mystery, and, of course, the corsetry.

As with the Javiera Collection, I had styled the girls in a highly feminine yet powerful way. With bold red lips and regal hair, they stood like queens and goddesses, like the legends they were meant to be.

And the fashion press? They approved. They gave me the perfect Valentine.

"Inspired by her heritage—her mother is Greek and her father Egyptian—Fotini ... looked to Cleopatra, Helen of Troy and Queen Nefertiti for her collection. There were laser-cut leather dresses, Grecian draped gowns, a snake-embellished little frock and delicate lace dresses, all worked with a feminine hand."

—WWD

"What would the ancient queens such as Cleopatra and Helen of Troy wear if they were alive today, asks Fotini? The answer lies in her collection. Based upon a palette of rich amber, tobacco, Bordeaux, mallard green and eggplant hues, Fotini's gowns, coats and dresses feature a mix of textiles. Her combinations of feathers with lace and chiffon with jacquard give the clothes an unexpected modern edge ... simultaneously feminine, powerful and timeless."

—Haute Diary

"Fotini Channels Her Inner Goddess From Her Heritage"
—International Business Times

"Fotini's Fall 2012 Collection was stunning, to say the least. Inspired by a perfume bottle that she inherited from an ancient Egyptian queen's tomb, Fotini designed a collection of dresses that were luxurious and opulent, hinting at royalty and exquisite dedication to the craft."

—Lady and the Blog

"The collection exudes luxury, femininity and class without being intimidating or overpowering ... Her pieces can easily become classic staples of any evening wardrobe, while also offering unique, modern and striking elements that will have heads turning in the wearer's direction."

—*Examiner*

The press had come out in full force. The show was a bona fide success.

No one knew how hard it had been for me at the rehearsal, the panic I felt when I looked up at the big stage and saw my own name up in lights. I had been thrilled to see FOTINI on the designer listings boards in the lobby, but in bright lights? I didn't like seeing that. I think that as much as I had feared failure, I now feared success and the risk of gaining it only to have it taken away.

Backstage before the presentation was all organized chaos, overwhelming for a relative novice. There were areas for hair, makeup, and snacks for the models as far as you could see. Designers and stylists were busy making sure each model was wearing the right dress with the assigned accessories. Allison was amazing, impressing me with her efficiency, organizing everyone like a drill sergeant.

When the presentation ended, I felt relief, pleasure, and the glow of a job well-done. As I congratulated my entire team, I felt a surge of pride in them, in myself, and in the choices I had made. Jacques Rossi. Allison Hart. Grace Tsui, keeping on top of her work, soothing my fears that she might be overwhelmed. My team's visions were often much the same (Allison) and occasionally conflicting (Jacques), but we had created something that was amazing, original, and real. I remember walking back to the apartment after the show. It was raining, so I'd put on my little rain boots. I thought I felt numb from the chilly weather, but when I got home, I realized it was from sheer exhaustion.

Later that evening, my family and some very close friends went back to Cipriani Downtown for a celebratory dinner. It felt wonderful being surrounded by warmth and love, even more so because my mother, father, my daughter Georgia, and her then boyfriend Lucas were there. They had flown in from Toronto to witness my collection's onstage success. My father, the man who had been opposed to my following a path to fashion when I'd been younger, was bursting with pride on that Valentine's Day.

I was also relieved. As a newcomer to NYFW, I went into Lincoln Center only hoping some powerful retailers might come to view the collection. I was especially happy that two fashion gurus had attended my presentation: Linda Fargo, senior VP of the fashion office and director of women's fashion and store presentation for Bergdorf Goodman, and Ken Downing, senior VP and fashion director at Neiman Marcus Stores.

This time, post-presentation, instead of setting up a showroom in my own studio, I elected to present the collection to buyers at Fleur Atelier, an independent showroom recommended to us by David Randall. Owned by a Frenchman, Alain Marchand, who was as elegant and tasteful as the loft-style showroom itself, this was the perfect space for the FOTINI brand.

Alain was selective and had once worked with the late, great Bill Blass. His space was rustic and chic: guests walked off a two-person elevator to Dyptique candles, fresh flowers, and French music playing.

Soon after New York Fashion Week, Sara invited me to Houston. During her visit months earlier to view the Javiera Collection, she had spoken to me about flying in for a trunk show, my first ever. She had, unfortunately, committed to another designer to present for that season, but said firmly, "For your next collection, I want you there for two days!" Now, she booked me for that two-day trunk show to present Autumn/Winter 2012, and she made an excellent suggestion by asking me to bring part of Spring/Summer 2012 as well, in order to fully showcase the FOTINI brand and show her clientele how special it was. I was elated. The time had now come.

Based on Autumn/Winter 2012's success following the success of Spring/Summer 2012's, I could now go in front of these women with credibility behind me, having acquired some traction as a New York designer with a special niche. My sales would be limited, however. Sara couldn't buy more than five of any single piece from me, so strong was her clients' fear that they might bump into someone else wearing the same thing.

Fashionable women want to be unique. Even a socialite who once bought an item saying, "You should be asking double what you charge," told me she wasn't interested if the chosen piece had already been sold to someone else in town. Giving top clients first choice and even exclusivity was marketing magic, even if it limited sales.

I had attended trunk shows as a client, but as the featured designer the tables were reversed and I had to prove myself, earn the respect of the clients. The fashion world of Houston was a very wide world away from that of New York. First, Sara hosted a beautiful lunch. This was no casual get-together: the sales staff went through training before the show so they would know how to describe the special fabrics and the craftsmanship. Because the garments were an investment, part of my role was to convince them that they could wear pieces for special occasions, or for travel, not just once. I was pleased and surprised to find that, in addition to my expected younger clientele, I had women in their sixties and seventies coming to me for corsets.

During coffee and dessert, the show began. I was a little nervous—these women weren't just potential customers, but could make or break a new designer.

I had two models showing the clothes. When choosing models, I had to be fussy about body types, because I couldn't afford to make multiple samples. (And by "afford," I mean that literally on a business level, as it would have put me way over budget.) In Houston, it was all about embracing femininity, and I wanted the clients to see a model that represented them as women. Because I used local models, I sometimes had to squeeze them into the garments. But they looked terrific. Following the presentation—and three standing ovations— the clients started trying things on. Then the salespeople came in to take care of their particular clients' orders. Pulling it all together was fabulous, if exhausting. I was on my knees pinning and hemming, and the women were shocked. They couldn't believe I did it myself! To me, it was both natural and important for me to do it. Why? Because the clients were so happy to connect with me in such a personal way. And because so much champagne had flowed at lunch, the stories started flowing too. Personal lives, personal struggles. Fashion isn't just decoration, it's the intimacy of women's lives.

Not everyone on staff took a shine to me at first, but even the seasoned saleswoman with the "Okay, impress me" attitude and the younger guy who appeared threatened by my trying to keep his customers happy ended up being two of my favorite people once they realized my dedication and commitment to hard work. In the end, the entire staff loved FOTINI.

In one way, Houston wasn't so different from New York after all—in fashion, no matter where you are, you have to prove yourself. And for me personally, you have to be yourself. It was a chance to bond, but it could also be risky. With women of all ages and shapes trying on my corseted pieces, I had to be honest about what would and wouldn't work for each woman. I couldn't be myself in any other way, and the upside was that the women were happy to get such personal attention from the designer and to find a great fit in striking clothing. Many had never owned or even tried on a corset, or clothing built around corsetry before. They were entranced with the way their body was molded into the pieces, the way it made them look. Fit is everything. It is the silver lining of molding the body.

It was the beginning of a great relationship, and the beginning of Sara's trust. The trunk show lasted two days. On the second day, I was wearing a suit from my first collection—a pearl-colored corset, woven jacquard skirt, and bolero jacket with beautiful pearl beading on the cuffs.

"There's going to be a pageant girl coming in," Sara informed me. "Her mother is one of my good friends and she won't be here, so I'm in charge."

The girl was around eighteen. She arrived in UGGs, sweatpants, and a tank top, her blonde hair in a ponytail. "Listen to me, young lady," Sara said maternally. "We are not going to go crazy. We're buying a suit."

The girl kept staring at me. She would try on one thing, stare, then take it off and try on another. After trying on several options, she finally said, "I want all that." She was pointing directly at me. She wanted everything I was wearing—the shoes, the jewelry, and most of all, the suit.

It was feminine and a great tailored fit to the body. The pageant girl bought the outfit, head to toe, and in the dressing room, Sara had to stop her from interrogating me on where I'd gotten all my jewelry. We made the suit to the appropriate length and measurements for a respected contestant, so it would please the senior advisors who would interview her. Later, when I received a photograph of her on the day of her interview, I smiled at how fabulous she looked.

This would be the beginning of a great business relationship. Sara understood her clientele and kept them happy. She would even go to clients' homes and organize their closets—a clever way to suggest filling in gaps in the clients' wardrobes or replacing clothes that were outdated.

I learned a lot from selling to Sara's store. It took me a while, but I found out that small boutiques, and retailers in general, will try to push the cost of alterations and unsold merchandise back onto the designer. Customers would ask for changes and the store would send the piece back to me, expecting me to make them. It would be two collections before I felt confident enough to push back and say that I couldn't do alterations for free. And when I did, my statement was gracefully accepted.

In May, I decided it was time to part ways with my second PR company. Unfortunately, like the first group, they simply were not bringing in a return on the investment: it was time to move on.

And then, just a few days later, the phone rang in the studio. It was from my now former public relations agency, calling to tell me perhaps the most impactful news of my New York fashion career.

"The Met Gala! What do you mean, the Met Gala?"

"The Met Gala! What do you mean, *the Met Gala?"* I was stunned beyond comprehension.

The biggest event in the American fashion world. I could barely process what I was hearing, even as the PR representative explained that this was actually happening. Nothing in the entire fashion world could compare to the Met Gala. It wasn't unusual for designers to wait years to have a celebrity choose an item from their line for the Met Gala. For a newcomer like me, it was astonishing.

It was something the public relations group had been working on. Now none other than Amy Poehler wanted to wear my FOTINI Cleopatra gown to fashion's most important event.

Let me put this in perspective. I had just presented only my second collection. Amy Poehler and her *Saturday Night Live* cohort Tina Fey were not only two of the hottest stars of television, they were comedic *royalty*. For Amy to want to wear one of my designs to *the* fashion gala of the year was a very, very big deal.

Before any important event, PR companies are on the phone promoting their fashion designer clients to stylists, editors, and agents. They are busy sending images of the collection, as well as sample gowns, to women who will be in the spotlight. It often comes to naught, with the celebrity choosing someone else's work from the broad selection. Now Amy Poehler had chosen FOTINI.

And now a new challenge began. Unlike established designers, I couldn't afford to make extra sample sizes I might be stuck with. So the delicate laser-cut leather that had been fitted on a six-foot-tall teenage model had to be altered to fit a real woman.

I didn't care how hard it was going to be or how fast we had to do it. I was going to make this work. The end decision had been Amy's and out of all the gowns she had seen—most of them from high-profile runway stars—she had chosen mine. She'd wanted something fashion forward that would make her look feminine yet edgy. She loved wearing a New York designer, so had chosen FOTINI.

We sent the finished dress over to her people the day of the event, and sure enough, as I was watching the live Met Gala coverage on my iPad that night, there was Amy Poehler looking radiant in the Cleopatra gown, all laser-cut leather and feathers, like a goddess. As the designer, I could see that her stylist had, unbeknownst to me, made a few minor alterations so the gown would fit perfectly. This isn't unusual when the designer doesn't do the final fitting.

Amy was photographed up and down the red carpet, and she took time on camera to say how much she loved her cutting-edge leather FOTINI gown.

"I'm thrilled to be getting to wear [FOTINI] tonight … and leaving a trail," the comedienne said of the sweetheart-neckline gown, fashioned of modern leather and featuring a whimsical feathered mermaid silhouette. Hearing those words while curled up on my couch at home with a glass of Frog's Leap Sauvignon Blanc made me very emotional, and I shed tears of joy and loneliness. It brought back the happiness mixed with sadness that had marked the period of my childhood when I was with my grandparents in Greece, cared for but still bereft at the absence of my parents. Here I was, with this monumental event happening, and yet I was alone, all by myself, with no one to share it. The fashion industry can be very lonely.

Still, I was over the moon. And the press kept rolling in.

"BEST DRESSED!"

—Perez Hilton

"FROM RUNWAY TO RED CARPET AT THE MET BALL"

—The Wall Street Journal

"Scene City: Will Arnett in Calvin Klein Collection and Amy Poehler in Fotini"

—The *New York Times*

"Amy Poehler in long black dress by Fotini"

—*Vogue Spain*

I hired another PR firm quickly: as a new designer especially, you can't afford to go without public relations for long. I didn't want the momentum to falter. This time we chose to go with a boutique company that was brand-new and an owner who had vowed to take on few clients, no more than she could truly stay on top of. To start, she had me host a luncheon at the famed Lambs Club, inviting about twenty editors and stylists who could be key connections. This immediately put me on the right track for more exposure. I presented a small fashion show so the editors could see the clothes up close; they were able to touch them and feel the fine quality of the fabric and see the fineness of the work. Each guest was gifted with a silk chiffon Javiera print scarf as a thank you, nestling in a pretty white box tied with silver ribbon, the FOTINI brand colors. Amazingly, this was the first time anyone in public relations had suggested an event like this to me.

The Lambs Club was also special for me because as I was led to my table for lunch at another time in the same period, I passed one of my idols, Carolina Herrera. Just spotting this epitome of elegance and style—a favorite with first ladies since her debut collection in

1981—was awesome. I could only hope to be a legend like her one day, but in the meantime I enjoyed the thought that now *I* was a New York designer, too.

It soon became increasingly clear that the boutique agency, while putting in the promised time for us, did not understand luxury or how to promote it. Nor did the owner have the kinds of connections she had claimed to have. Everyone talked big, I now realized, but few people could deliver.

As I searched for a fourth PR company, Christina Moretti, who had led me to Allison, told me that she had friends I should talk to: Liv and Ann, who had a company called MediaMode Communications. Liv ran the business side of things, and Ann was on the front lines, running sales. In October we hired them, and they immediately got to work. Both excelled at what they did: Liv was smart, solid, and connected, while Ann was a professional schmoozer with good instincts and the most engaging smile.

We also reevaluated our relationship with David Randall, and as 2012 was drawing to a close, we decided, after careful consideration, that we didn't need the consulting firm's services any longer. Certainly not when we were paying the same monthly retainer as a major international retailer client of theirs—one with much deeper pockets.

I had learned so much through this fall collection, but I was already immersed in Spring/Summer 2013. I had already decided upon the vision and inspiration of this next collection, already started the mood boards, already gone through the Pantone books choosing color palettes.

I needed to focus on this collection, not just for the obvious reasons of realizing my dreams and advancing my business, but to distract me from a crisis that could threaten the new collection. Barbara needed orthopedic surgery. Coming in from New Jersey three or even four times a week was wearing on her, and her mobility had decreased to the point that her doctor had ordered surgery. This affected me deeply, because I genuinely cared for her. In fact, in spite of her being difficult at times, she was the first person I hired when opening my studio and had treated me like a daughter. I was happy she would be healthier after surgery. But it posed a daunting problem I would need to deal with. The timing was dreadful. Soon I would have no production lead.

There was no way, on such a tight schedule, that I could bring in someone who didn't intimately know and understand the brand. The production lead role is key. It's a vital part of the team. Having the wrong person could prove disastrous. That meant Gino and I would have to lead the production houses in addition to performing our own roles. We were in for more than I ever could have imagined. I was anxious, and the seemingly endless New York winter wasn't calming me down.

I worried and fretted day and night, trying either to come up with a solution or not think about it at all. Neither happened. The gray, sullen weather was not helping my mood, or quelling my fears. Still, as winter wore on, I noted more frequent shafts of morning light slipping in through the studio windows. It soothed me with a softness that reminded me of another place, another time, a period free from worry.

Years ago, on a trip to Provence, I had awoken and looked outside to see nothing but sunlight and blooming wisteria. I'd been carrying that image around in my mind for years. I loved the way the wisteria hung, delicate and exquisite. I hadn't known what I would do with those images I carried so close to my heart—until they had inspired the collection on which I now worked. Now, as I sketched designs, looked at materials, and thought about silhouettes, I resolved to leave my fears behind and lose myself in that dream of France.

For now, I told myself, I must focus on this, just this. This place and time, this collection, would be my refuge for now: sunlight, flowers in bloom, the gentle caress of spring breezes. If I wanted to have a collection at all, I had to ignore the storm clouds gathering above my head.

I would not, could not, think about what lay ahead. I didn't dare.

CHAPTER EIGHT
Dances of Joy

Look for the opportunities in the
challenges that come to you.
—FOTINI

The visions of those lush flowering vines outside my window in Provence consumed me, especially the appealing colors of the blooms: ambrosial shades of violet, purple, white, and pink. Like the macarons in the French patisserie I would visit in the mornings. The colors of confections.

What resonated even more with me was wisteria's personality. Its delicate, often sweetly scented flowers sprang from immensely strong vines. I loved the way they fell like romantic teardrops.

From this glorious holiday, I had tucked away the thought of creating something special one day: a representation of how much this wisteria plant had resonated with me. And so the time had finally come, and my Spring/Summer 2013 collection was going to embrace my wisteria story and the splendors of France.

The Wisteria of France Collection.

My inspiration did not stop there—the muted color palette of eighteenth century French painters chimed in. Watteau, Boucher, and Fragonard used delicate colors to create sumptuous looks. The palette for this collection was butter, sage, soft pink, lavender, taupe, pale baby blue, and white, straight from the canvas of a rococo painting. The epitome of romance and femininity.

Made for the woman of elegance and grace with an element of mystery and playfulness. For someone who might imagine she is sitting for Fragonard to immortalize her in his famed painting *The Swing*.

There was an explosion of inspiration on the mood boards. The collection also had to represent France. Women in chic Paris street style, Impressionist paintings, butter-colored *crème caramel* desserts, and colorful Versailles-style *jardins* were the images we focused on. The custom FOTINI print this season was Wisteria—created in two color ways, one in pink, sage, and butter and the other in blue, magenta, and lavender.

I was kicking off with a new team. Jennifer had left to go back to Ralph Lauren. She recommended Vanessa Gallo as her replacement, and what a recommendation! I will forever be grateful to her. Barbara was in recovery now. Even the lightest, frothiest garments are created through a challenging process and after her complicated surgery, my fear was confirmed: Barbara would face a long healing process. It was too late to fill the gap. From a production standpoint, my team and I were on our own for Spring/Summer 2013.

There were other team issues, as well. It happens. People get demanding, people become needy, people have personal problems, people let their moods affect the others. This is all part of a diverse group of personalities. Some of my closest team members, on whom I depended so greatly and who were such close friends, could be a challenge at times. But we were really scrambling now and all of us were anxious, so I made only the most necessary changes.

My team meant everything to me and was part of my lifeline for this brand—these glorious creations that I dreamed and designed in my mind came to life through their dedicated and loyal efforts. Never take for granted the loyalty of those who really care.

Happily, we had struck gold with the new PR team. At their suggestion, we took on such strategic high-profile events as the Botanical Garden Gala in December of 2012, and the Museum of the City of New York Gala sponsored by Carolina Herrera in February. The goal was to give FOTINI exposure and secure presence in the New York fashion world. I was meeting journalists, senior executives, socialites, celebrities—always keeping in mind that the goal was to dress them. I was featured in *Manhattan, Scene, Harper's Bazaar,* and *Cosmopolitan*—where Kendall Jenner wore my Anais blouse and Jeannette short. Yes, the FOTINI brand was getting traction and being noticed. At last the power of the right public relations team was paying off for me!

FOTINI was being talked about and had the right buzz around the brand. Like wisteria, a blossoming force in the fashion world. I had taken a giant step forward into the world I'd always longed to be a part of, the one I was determined to conquer.

The collection was set apart by a leap into some daring experiments that showed FOTINI the brand wasn't only about gowns and "occasion dressing." On the streets of Paris, a woman might wear jeans and a T-shirt, but everything would be put together beautifully each time and paired off with the right accessories: a hat, a scarf, a pair of sunglasses, or a pair of carefully chosen shoes. The embodiment of chic.

For me, it was always vital that the look seen on the platform or runway was actually "the" look. Some designers design and choose accessories not to indicate how the look should be worn in real life, but to send an artistic message. I chose to be more pragmatic, to showcase each item in my collections in a realistic and wearable version. When a woman walks out the door, what story is she telling the world?

Women must always remember: you wear the clothes—the clothes don't wear you.

Shorts were a risk and an experiment for me, but I couldn't imagine not including them in this collection. The color choices were white, pink, and butter. These polished, tailored Jeannette shorts, paired with a stunning Wisteria print blouse with Swarovski buttons or a silk chiffon and Chantilly lace cami, were flirtatious, yet still as soft and feminine as the rest of the collection. Fresh and modern.

I chose stilettos to elongate the leg, but even if I'd shown the shorts with stylish flats, the look would have been chic and current. It was important to me to offer women different looks and ideas of how to wear the garments. Especially when you are building and investing in your wardrobe, you need to be versatile.

And the Wisteria of France Collection offered women streamlined versatility from the clean and crisp white corded cotton Angelique dress to the pleated Lilliane taupe gauze corset, which stood on its own or as an underpinning of the Nicole suit.

I had a soft spot in my heart for the short, flirty Calli and Georgia cocktail dresses—the Calli with its embroidered Wisteria appliqué on silk organza, and the Georgia with a dazzling rose, beaded embellishment on silk chiffon. In every collection, my sketches/designs, or "my girls," as I called them, were named after my inspiration—in this case, with French names. There was always a Calli and a Georgia, the names of my daughters. It made me feel like they were there with me every time, close to me.

Lincoln Center's The Box was where I had chosen to show Spring/Summer 2013 on September 13, 2012. After exceptional attention and heavy traffic of attendees for Autumn/Winter 2012, I decided this was clearly the place to be. The presentation format in that setting had proven to be in my best interest for showcasing the collection. Plus, the press, editors, bloggers, retailers, and other influencers showed up there to see well-established names. Lincoln Center had them: Oscar de la Renta, Monique Lhuillier, Ralph Lauren, Carolina Herrera, and more. These designers were enormous draws and those who attended their shows were top tier decision makers.

The models posed on platforms at the center of a carefully assembled French-inspired garden, filled with greens and fresh lavender that complemented the delectable hues of the fabrics and transported viewers to a lighthearted world. The total effect was like entering a dream, a fairy tale, a beautiful painting.

Not surprisingly, one favorite would be the empowering Camille tuxedo in cady, a slightly stretchy georgette with a silk faille lapel; this soon became a frequent request for both brides and bridesmaids. Another was the ethereal corseted silk chiffon Wisteria print Emmanuelle gown with its thigh-high slit, celebrated by the media for its unique blend of daring and demure.

"Hues of butter, sage, soft pink, lavender, taupe and white make these dresses perfect for summer weddings and outdoor celebrations."

—Scene Magazine

"Fotini held an intimate presentation filled with light and airy frocks, all with French sensibility."

—WWD

"Her collection speaks not to one woman but to all women."

—Style To Envy

The Javiera Collection, my first, had been strong and mysterious with an element of seduction. My second, Egyptian Queens and Greek Goddesses, was opulent and powerful. Wisteria of France, my third and now my largest, was enchanting, feminine, and playful—for the woman in control. Yes, I was speaking to all women.

During Market Week, we featured the collection to buyers at Fleur Atelier for a second time. For a designer with my aesthetic, the ambience of class, sophistication, and elegance was very important, but we soon discovered that Alain lacked two vital attributes. A designer doesn't pay just for the space—the space's owner is also responsible for promoting the line. Anyone promoting a new designer needs both passion and drive, and Alain simply lacked the hustle, the enthusiasm, and commitment I was looking for in a salesperson.

Thankfully, the orders were coming in; I was present for some appointments so I could personally sell FOTINI.

And then, as I was rushing to be at Fleur Atelier, shrugging off anxieties about staffing—especially what to do about Barbara—yet thrilled with the reception for my beloved Wisteria of France, a call came in that I could never have expected. Houston Fashion Week was inviting FOTINI to be one of the featured designers, and it was going to be a runway show.

I was caught so off-guard that I wasn't sure how to respond. "Thank you, I'm very flattered," I told the representative at the other end of the line. "I have to check schedules, but I will get back to you right away."

Sara Peters, along with her clients who were admirers and wore FOTINI proudly, had recommended to the senior executives at Houston Fashion Week that the FOTINI brand be included in this grand show.

Why wouldn't I answer immediately? I wasn't trying to play hard to get. I just had to be sure. My first thought was, *How am I going to pay for all this?* In discussions around NYFW runway versus presentation format, I had always opted for presentation not only as the right choice for my brand, but also because I was aware of the astronomical costs of doing a runway show. I had a budget and I was determined to stick to it. Too many designers fade early or lose control of their brand by not doing so.

As it turned out, an even better surprise was awaiting me: I didn't have to pay for everything!

Vanessa and I did a little dance of joy when we were told that the space, hair, and makeup, and even the models, would be paid for by the invitees buying expensive tickets. A welcome response indeed! With a sigh of relief, I saw that my expenses would be limited to transportation of FOTINI team members with the collection, hotel accommodations, and any personal costs. HFW was relatively new but already attracting well-known designers like Zac Posen, Herve Leger, BCBG by Max Azria, and Monique Lhuillier. These were names synonymous with glamour and class. It felt right. Houston, here I come.

The models were pre-chosen by the HFW team after being given the sample size of the collection. While this was a welcome gesture, it did prove to have its challenges. These were not the models I had made the collection for, and therefore Allison and I had to work some magic to make everything fit perfectly.

As a designer, you have presentation models and fit models. The presentation models are the ones that are in the show at Fashion Week, chosen from the hundreds of girls who come to the castings. The fit model is the model used in production of the collection. This model is typically the more realistic in size, closer to the size of the women who will be buying the clothes. While presentation models are usually size 0-2, a fit model can range from a size 6-10. A pattern is made for that size and then "graded." The grading system is a necessary step that must be taken before approaching sample manufacturers or production houses. Card sets are required of the designer's patterns and an order of the garments to be produced. The grading system allows you to have a variety of sizes for each garment and fills your minimum order cost effectively. Essentially, it allows the producers and manufacturers to increase or decrease the size of the original shape, the size the fit model is.

Vanessa, Allison, and I were in heaven when we arrived with the collection and found that, true to their word, the people at HFW had taken care of everything. When I first saw that long, long runway, I was still momentarily fazed. It's sobering when you see just how far the models will have to walk in their stratospheric heels. But I hadn't come this far without believing I could achieve whatever I set my mind to.

The collection was perfectly suited for a runway show, with fabrics that fluttered and swirled as the models moved. At rehearsal I was pinching myself. Was this really happening, a runway show? Something new to me had been selecting the right music for runway and overseeing the choreography to be sure the models walked to the beat. I worked endlessly in New York with a professional, coming up with a fabulous collection of music—that being said, there were no guarantees that it would all come together.

Once again, I was haunted by seeing my name in the largest sign at the top of the runway.

FOTINI.

"This is so exciting, Fotini," Allison said with delight.

"Yes, it is," I responded, even as a wave of fear swept over me.

How long would it last?

Shouldn't I be ecstatic and beaming? I wondered. I was, but I could not quite bask in the delight of what was about to happen that evening.

"Fotini, I want you to come out at the end of the show and wave, present yourself and your accomplishment of this fabulous collection. Maybe do a little dance," said Allison.

Vanessa and I burst out laughing, knowing very well that showcasing myself was not my style. I thought of Betsey Johnson and the wonderful cartwheels she would do at the end of her shows. But she was Betsey Johnson. And I was me. And that meant I would simply walk out and graciously acknowledge the applause. And so Tuesday, November 13th, 2012, at 8:30 p.m., showtime arrived!

Allison, Vanessa, and I were ready, run of show—the detailed show schedule—was ready and set, thanks to Allison's diligent and authoritative role with the models and Vanessa's labeling the shoes with each model's outfit and size and lining up all the sunglasses, which were the perfect accessory.

For my HFW debut I chose to wear the Brigitte cocktail dress, of iridescent lamé with a beaded floral appliqué.

"Showtime! Let's go, girls!" I exclaimed.

And so it began: the music, rushing back for the next look, different clothes, different shoes, a change of accessories. Yes, it was chaos, but blood-rushing, invigorating chaos. I loved it!

Silently, I was chanting, *Don't trip! Don't trip!* The three of us were saying our prayers as we stared at the runway, all eighty feet of it being stalked by strong but delicate-looking models in six- and seven-inch heels. How could I not be a little nervous?

The girls were all amazing. The silky fabrics of the dresses and gowns swayed and shimmered like froth. And my last look, the Marie Antoinette gown, with its corseted fit and beaded flounces, was a showstopper, a creation beyond my expectations. As if to add to the suspense, the model who was to wear it for the finale had fainted and fallen in the show before mine. So it was a huge relief to see that not only was she okay and recovered, but that she walked out there and owned that runway.

Sara Peters was in the front row with her select group of clients and senior staff. When I came out and waved after the parade of models for the finale, I received a standing ovation, attendees clapping and showing their appreciation for FOTINI. I was elated; I felt so much joy and such a sense of accomplishment that words could not express my emotions.

My triumph was bittersweet, though. As much as Vanessa and Allison were like family now and a great comfort to me, the fact remained that none of my immediate family had come. There were valid reasons, plus it was a long way to Texas and I would barely have had time to see them. And yet I couldn't help but feel like the little girl who had landed the lead in the "seven swans a swimming category" for the Christmas play *The Twelve Days of Christmas.* No one had shown up then either.

On one level, it was fine. I compartmentalized well. The next day was a new day and the first of my two-day trunk show at Sara's store. I absolutely loved working with my customers, helping them with their wardrobe looks, introducing items they would shy away from before being won over. My collections were always for the woman who is confident. The Houston women themselves were delightful. They were colorful, and sometimes they were demanding, yet I took such pleasure in seeing them and sharing stories.

One of my best customers was a senior executive at a prestigious corporation, a petite force of nature who worked in a very male-dominated environment. "Fotini, when I wear your brand, it commands the right attention. I feel powerful yet feminine, and I like to be noticed," she said. This woman was not one who suffered fools well and yet she shared some of her personal challenges with me. The loyalty went both ways. I sold my little heart out over the course of two days with Vanessa by my side filling out every order, making sure all the i's were dotted and t's crossed. We worked hard and were finally ready to get back to New York, both satisfied and exhausted.

As the plane landed at LaGuardia Airport, I found myself saying in my mind, *Home. Where is home?*

The next day it was business as usual. I was to attend an event I had been looking forward to, the New Yorkers for Children Fall Gala. At the suggestion of my PR company, I had purchased five seats at a table for the dinner. It was a serious fashion crowd—not just designers but editors, actors, and other VIPs—for a wonderful cause. I was very excited at the opportunity to meet colleagues and further introduce FOTINI the brand and the person. I wore my Isis gown from Autumn/Winter 2012 and met my PR advisor at the famous Cipriani on Fifth Avenue, a frequent venue for special events.

After my photo op on the red carpet, we moved toward our table. I was thrilled when I saw that a very hot handbag designer, who was now designing clothes and had just opened her own store in SoHo, was seated there. Upon our introduction, my excitement quickly evaporated. She shook my hand in a perfunctory way while looking me up and down, awkward and somewhat rude.

"It's a pleasure to meet you," I said, remaining pleasant and professional.

"Is that one of yours?" she asked icily, with a nod to my gown.

"Yes, it is," I proudly answered.

"So you design—what—gowns?" Her tone was arrogant.

"Yes," I replied. "Gowns, cocktail dresses, suits...."

That was it. My voice trailed off as she disappeared into the crowd, returning to the table only to eat and converse with the person she came with. After dinner we lost her again. I had imagined she would be lovely, so her attitude disappointed and surprised me. What I walked away with that evening is that I did connect and meet lovely people and all for a wonderful charity, and that being kind doesn't cost anything. I was proud to be the person I am, someone who competed with herself and didn't resent others.

The only person you need to compete with and raise the bar for is you.

I had a totally different experience when I went to Monique Lhuillier's boutique opening on Madison Avenue. That was a genuine pleasure. A crowd of celebrities and media representatives had shown up to see the one of the Queens of Bridal's gorgeous New York store and see her newly launched ready-to-wear collection. Monique was a celebrity in her own right, who has since gone on to collections including evening gowns, linens, and, in collaboration with Waterford, tableware—and she could not have been more gracious. My PR representative, Liv, who knew Monique, and I arrived a little early. Before all the chaos began, she took us on a personal tour, ignoring the waiting photographers and editors until I finally said,

"You don't have to be here with me when so many people are waiting for you." She was sheer class.

The following day, it was back to FOTINI reality at the studio, where not everything had gone smoothly. Still, I had shown at NYFW, taken orders to fill, attended my first HFW and a major trunk show, and somehow we had survived the production of this collection. *Barely.*

Once again, with team effort not only from my staff, but from my production houses and seamstresses, we'd made it happen. Gino had really stepped up to the plate as the liaison with the suppliers when I could not be present and even when I was, proving again that the right team members make all the difference.

In the midst of all this, I found out that one of my dreams was about to come true.

Ever since I can remember, *Vogue* was the bible of fashion. As a little girl, I watched many women reading it. So, even before I was actually producing collections, I knew that anyone who followed fashion recognized the magazine as the *crème de la crème* of publications.

I couldn't hit the speaker button fast enough when Ann from MediaMode called me at the studio and shrieked in delight, "Fotini, we have an appointment with *Vogue*!" Vanessa and Gino were wide-eyed as she went on, "They want to look at several pieces from your collections!"

"I'll be ready, Ann," I said, bursting with anticipation as she relayed the details. As a team, we were beyond grateful to be called in, but personally

As I did the "dance of joy" in the studio, all I could think was that Vogue *wanted to see me!*

I had the added emotion of my usual blend of nerves and excitement. As I did the "dance of joy" in the studio, all I could think was that

Vogue wanted to see me!

We gathered all the pieces my PR group had asked for me to bring, carefully steaming every piece, checking every stitch and ensuring that they were spotless. The next day we prepared the items for travel as carefully as if we were wrapping priceless Impressionist paintings. After that, Ann and I, along with our roller racks, got into one of the many white garment vans that are a common sight in midtown Manhattan. As we were approaching the Condé Nast Building, I felt a little sick, butterflies fluttering like never before.

I remember entering the building with the collections on the roller racks, and as we got through the tight security and into the elevator, looking at the directory list of all the top magazines in this building. *Condé Nast.* This was literally a dream coming true: for anyone in the fashion industry, this was indeed their playground.

When we arrived on the meeting floor, we were asked to take a seat in the elevator bank lobby where all the initial "designer" meetings take place.

What? We don't get to go through the glass doors where all the employees are going?

A little bit of my dream changed into reality with that realization. It wasn't glamorous at all. There were several of us waiting there: a jewelry designer, beauty representative, fashion designer, fitness gadget inventor. It was each of our dreams to be somehow associated with the one and only *Vogue.*

After we had been waiting for an hour, the person we were supposed to see finally came out; she was both friendly and respectful, but barely apologized for being late before turning to the collection. I was grateful that she looked over each garment twice and attentively, taking care as she handled them. And I was gratified to hear that she was so impressed by everything I wanted to be known for—the construction, finishing, and fabrics. But I couldn't help feeling let down by the lack of glamour on that floor at least. Through the glass doors leading to the halls of the inner sanctum, I could see the staff. I could see that they weren't wearing couture clothes with Louboutin heels. This was not *The Devil Wears Prada*. This was very much like everywhere else in corporate America—I could have been back at Merrill Lynch. And yet, this *was* a dream and it *was* special and it *did* count! Because it was *VOGUE*! Sometimes dreams are not how you envisioned they would be. But *Vogue* was still *Vogue*.

One of my great sources of comfort during this period of mixed emotions, loneliness, and exhaustion was my little Yorkie, Bronx. My love for New York went far and deep for so many years that I had come up with a name before I had a dog, a name that was my personal tribute to this fabulous place. My four-and-a-half-pound hero has always lived up to his New York roots: he is feisty, funny, and captures your heart the moment you meet him—a blessing, though often a distraction.

Bronx accompanied me to the studio every day and made it his own, once panicking everyone at a meeting when he went under the fabric table to hide between rolls of fabric. I suspected he wasn't getting enough attention. We feared he'd somehow fallen off the balcony until we found him staring back at us with typical New York City insouciance, looking as if he had accomplished his goal—attention on him!

Now, as I was about to go into my fourth collection, the stress of balancing travel, family, and staff issues, was slowly escalating. At this point I was living in New York seventy-five percent of my time. This was the necessary sacrifice that had to be made.

Some very key decisions were now due. Replacing Alain and Fleur Atelier as a showroom. Replacing Barbara, who could not commit to the commute from New Jersey or the rigorous work after her surgery. A new production lead was the most important. We simply could not go through another collection without that role. *Could not, would not.*

We had put out the word in the Garment District that we were looking for a production lead. This is not an easy role to fill if you want an expert. When a referral came through Grace Tsui, in whom I had great trust, my hopes skyrocketed.

Could this woman, Juliet Walsh, be the answer to our prayers—the brilliant production savior we needed?

In the meantime, the continued promotion of the Wisteria Collection was also at the forefront. Ideas for Autumn/Winter 2013 were flowing. Alone in New York with little Bronx, I started to work on silhouettes and mood boards. Homesick for not only family but any kind of familiarity, at night in my apartment I would recall Monique Lhuillier's words at her store opening. These were words of a successful designer who had reached the pinnacle after a decade of hard work.

"Fotini," she had told me honestly and passionately, "it's just so hard."

Is anything worthwhile in life accomplished without sacrifice, compromise, and total dedication?

The answer is no. Certainly not for me.

Is it worth the blood, sweat, and tears? Yes, yes, it is. Sometimes it is just so hard.

Did I have another collection in me? Was I up to the challenge? Just watch me!

Oh, there was one other thing happening then. My daughter Georgia was getting married! And she had asked me to design her gown. One more "dance of joy"—perhaps the most joyful of them all—was necessary.

CHAPTER NINE

The Empress and the Princess

Power and femininity are a
formidable combination.

—FOTINI

I had little time to celebrate the great success of the Wisteria of France Collection. Two very important women were awaiting me. The first was my daughter Georgia, depending on me to design a unique gown for her wedding. The second was Catherine the Great, Empress Catherine II of Russia, the powerful woman who was one of several inspirations for my Fall/Winter 2013 Romanov Collection.

Like all my collections, this too would be personal, focused on themes and images from an unforgettable 2003 trip to Russia, where I had been swept away by the extravagant beauty of the tsars and the empire, in particular the Amber Room of the palace of Catherine the Great at Tsarkoye Selo, just outside of St. Petersburg.

Catherine the Great was a tremendous force in bringing cultural and liberal reforms to Russia. A powerful and fascinating woman, intelligent and sensual, she captivated the citizens with charm, taste, and creativity that far outweighed her lack of conventional beauty. Already a favorite of the masses, she became the enlightened empress in a coup d'état that resulted in the abdication of her emperor husband in 1762.

I had the Romanovs, the ruling family of the tsars, in mind when I was taken on a special personal tour of the palace and discovered the room created out of amber, the dazzling mineral of distinctive orange, gold, and butter hues. As when I was a child, I have remained entranced by metallic colors, and walking into the lavish, ornate Amber Room was like entering a box of the most dazzling gold and bronze Crayola crayons. It was as if a childhood dream had come true.

The details were intoxicating and felt intensely powerful to me. The intricacy of the interior—the carvings and the embossed crests, the moldings, the brilliant craftsmanship—was so overwhelming. And yet I felt peaceful. I was transported to another era.

The color ways of this room, one of the most opulent rooms in history, transfixed me. So did other aspects of the great imperial city. Fabergé eggs had long been a passion of mine, starting from the time my father introduced me to their elaborate, mysterious beauty as a child. I went to the Hermitage, the enormous art and culture museum established by the empress in 1764, where I was saddened to learn that its renowned collection had been taken away for maintenance, but I still could see many awe-inspiring eggs for sale in the shops of St. Petersburg and Moscow at astronomical prices. Memories of that voyage never left me.

When I started thinking about Fall/Winter 2013, I thought of the greatest dynasty of a land synonymous with wintertime and of its empress and the Amber Room. How would I tell this story through FOTINI?

I thought of another of Russia's famous gems: malachite, the rich green mineral with its distinctive patterns.

All that was missing was modernity, and the Amber Room supplied the key.

I would take the malachite patterns without the traditional color. The color ways would stem from the Amber Room and my personal impressions of the empire. A designer, while not a grand empress, is the absolute ruler inside their own studio, holding the power to make the antique fresh and current.

I would take the luxuriant colors of amber to make the Romanov Collection my own. The mood boards pictured the gilded exterior of the palace and its glowing interior. Swatches of intensely colored fabrics were accompanied by yet more swatches: of beading, embroidery, lace, marquetry, even laces that were both bejeweled *and* beaded. Everything reflected the grandeur of the Romanovs.

And so the sketches began for the collection, but as important as they were, the design and vision for the signature print were imperative. We made several submissions to Ratti, now our partner for every FOTINI print. This one was going to be a version of malachite produced in two color ways and two fabrics. The first centered on shades of gray, black, and morel, contemporized in filmy silk chiffon. The other featured a combination of amber and navy in a structured krill fabric for a more regal look.

Every piece was steeped in history yet modern.

The Tanya corset of wool crepe with bullion and beaded embroidery.

The Raina cocktail dress of shimmering lurex lace, shining with metallic brilliance.

The Katerina gown with its frothing, full silk tulle ball gown skirt and velvet accents taking it to the Grand Event category.

The Elena suit of metallic red and morel silk jacquard.

The streamlined simplicity of the sleek, gleaming red leather Natalia dress with its exposed zipper.

The russet wool jacquard Lara dress with its two rows of ruffles, perfect at any casually elegant event.

The Valentina coat, a signature standout with its Romanovs print and Swarovski crystal buttons.

Even before I began, the collection presented me with a new challenge: finding a pattern maker/production house suited for this strong, structured collection. The brilliant Frenchman, Jacques Rossi, was ever so talented, but this collection required a different hand. I needed someone who was not afraid to cross boundaries with fabrics or delve into bringing modernization to this rich collection while remaining true to its royal aesthetic.

I found what I was looking for in Giancarlo. A true artist, Giancarlo was one of the key pattern makers for Vera Wang and other well-established fashion houses. His atelier was just across the courtyard from my studio, close enough that we could see into each other's windows. He was very territorial and private about allowing anyone new into his studio and therefore did not want me coming to him—he chose to come to me for our meetings. The fear of allowing just anyone into your studio in this very competitive industry is that they could steal your ideas and vision. I understood this maestro—he was that good—but I was somewhat offended at first. He did not know me nor I him, but I trusted and respected him and wanted that reciprocated. That came quickly as he got to know me, my brand,

and (in his words) the "magnificent" collection. I celebrated my own vision and artistry, taking inspiration from personal experiences. I did not need to take anyone else's. Sometimes accepting eccentricity as the cost of doing business is worth it. It was with Giancarlo.

I discovered firsthand how talented Giancarlo was when he came to my studio to see how I would look in the Emmanuelle gown (from the Wisteria Collection) that I planned to wear to my daughter's wedding. He shook his head. "The way the pleats fall, that will not show the best version of the corsetry." In his opinion, more room in the bust area was the key to the perfect fit. He made the adjustments—using Sofia Vergara's bust form which he worked from for my measurements—and the result was not only fantastic to look at but also more comfortable for me to wear. Giancarlo was like a brilliant maestro conducting his orchestra concert: the end result was music to one's ears.

I added another new person to the team, of course: Juliet Walsh. When Grace Tsui had recommended her to me, Juliet was on the verge of taking a break. But I managed to change her mind. Just as Barbara Marino had, Juliet told me she wanted to feel inspired and excited, that was what attracted her to FOTINI as a brand she could fully get behind. She embraced the luxury of FOTINI—the fine fabrics, the attention to finishing, the designs. Everyone in the industry respected Juliet, and she never disappointed me.

She was a gem beyond words, this amazing woman. And the whole team felt that way. She and Giancarlo worked well together. Fashion is a very small world, and both of them recognized the other's high level of talent. Tall and slim, with a striking Bohemian style, Juliet could have been a model. Beneath her soft, calming voice, she could be as tough as any military officer. You did not want to disappoint this woman. Not ever.

Juliet brought in her own assistant, Isabel, who was also fantastic. The two of them were exemplars of perfectionism, of getting things done. They accepted no excuses.

Did everyone accept Juliet immediately? No. When you bring in someone on that level, someone so respected that others in the industry were impressed that she was working with me, someone will always be envious or intimidated. But Juliet, with her soft-spoken voice and strict professionalism, was loved by almost all. It was hard not to love her, and it was impossible to deny that her choosing FOTINI meant the brand was out of the ordinary.

For this collection, I changed the presentation location to an intimate suite at the Pierre Hotel. Grand, formal, and elegant, it was the perfect spot, a New York legend and a place where the Romanovs would have felt at home. The suite was luxurious, and the presentation was distinctive, reminiscent of the old "by appointment" private showings. Garments were displayed on eight bust forms, as if in a museum or an art exhibition, and two live models would walk through wearing the different pieces for the guests to see. The presentation was for one day only, and we were busy from the first appointment at eight in the morning to the last at five in the afternoon.

Guests were generous in their admiration, the top editors for whom I created custom FOTINI corsets being especially pleased. I was gratified that the press and buyers responded to my vision of amber and malachite.

"The collection was breathtaking and kept me wanting more!"

—Exclusive Kat

"The Greek-Canadian designer is making strides to define her place in the annals of fashion history."

—Huffington Post

"Fotini kept her selections in...wearable territory without losing the drama: red leather, lace, and metallics."

—Houstonia magazine

After the New York presentation, the Romanov Malachite collection and I were off to FOTINI's season trunk show in Texas, where I faced a dilemma. As I mentioned previously, my experiences doing the trunk shows had taught me that plenty of wine and champagne flowed at these events and sometimes the women ended up a bit tipsy.

This was certainly the case with one Houston socialite who had imbibed freely and now wanted the Lydia red leather jacket—and was insistent that I make her a matching skirt in to go with it. This posed a bit of a conundrum. Was this suitable for her frame? If she changed her mind and declined the order, could I easily sell such a specialized piece? The red leather, pencil skirt would have been over the top for her once she really took notice.

I sought out Sara. "What should I do?" I asked worriedly. "She also wants the Collette dress for her daughter to wear at the Kentucky Derby but insists there's no reason to send a photo!"

"The daughter will be fine," Sara said, assuring me that she knew her and that she'd love the dress and look fabulous in it. "As for the skirt, tell her you'll order it. She has a tendency to do this and then bring things back, but I think I can change her mind before you make it."

Sure enough, it wasn't long before I heard from Sara: "I talked to her later and she said no skirt."

That was very good news. I can pull people out of their comfort zone to try something new, as I did when convincing a woman in her seventies that she would look beautiful in a FOTINI corset. (She looked great, and she knew it.) But I couldn't ever suggest or promote a look that wouldn't make my customer look anything but their best. It's not in my DNA.

On the subject of honesty, I learned a very important lesson on that trip to Houston. A customer who had become a corset enthusiast and who bought everything she liked whenever I came to Houston to show a collection was having marital troubles. I was told that her spending habits had been cut back quite a bit.

Now newly single, she was going to attend an art gallery opening that evening and desperately wanted to wear my laser-cut leather Cleo corset from the Fall/Winter 2012 collection. She wondered if she could "borrow" it and return it first thing the next day. I was uneasy, but Sara asked me to do her this favor, and in good faith I said yes. It was my only sample.

And the following day, day two of the trunk show, the fear I had suppressed was realized. She had not returned it.

"Sara," I said, politely but firmly, "you're going to have to call her and get her to return it." Eventually, it was recovered. But I'd learned a very important lesson: always trust your intuition.

To further liven things up around this time, New York got hit with Hurricane Sandy!

I had a corner apartment on the twenty-sixth floor that was practically all windows, which was glorious most times, during most seasons. I was cooking dinner for my visiting husband and little Bronx when the windows started shaking.

It was frightening, but we were very, very lucky. The storm eventually passed, but the damage was not easily rectified—I remember Gino had to go to the studio to get an internet connection, due to loss of power. The previous year, in September, I was working out in the gym when a freak snowstorm hit. As I ran on the treadmill, I looked up and saw that there was zero visibility outside. As during the hurricane, questions popped up in my mind. Would the power go out? Was it wiser to stay here than get in the elevator? A workout of descending fifty-seven flights of stairs wasn't what I had in mind.

I had a lot on my mind as it was, of course. When I wasn't thinking about the dramatic garments reflecting an empress, I was busy working on sketches for the romantic gown required by a princess. My daughter Georgia wanted a wedding dress rich in fairy-tale femininity. So many royals!

Romance had reigned ever since my future son-in-law, Georgia's boyfriend of five years or so, came to ask for my daughter's hand in marriage, a request joyfully granted. This was followed by Lucas proposing in New York while the two were on a getaway. The engagement was a year long, and it was a year filled with research and work for the bride-to-be and her mother.

My daughter and I went to several bridal stores so she could try on dresses. She tried on many gowns from Vera Wang to Amsale. For fun, we even went to Kleinfeld's with her best friend and soon-to-be mother-in-law who had flown in from Toronto. *Say Yes to the Dress* was being filmed, and she got the whole experience. It was valuable research, since before I might even begin to make suggestions or start sketches, I needed to know what silhouettes Georgia liked best. It was very important to me that it would capture who she was: in her early twenties, petite, fiery, and, yes, beautiful. It had to be a dress she would love, something uniquely her own that reflected her. What we came up with together was certainly one of a kind.

The materials were as luxurious as could be, from the yards and yards of silk tulle to the corded lace. A special touch was the horsehair bow. This was fashioned of yarn made from horse's hair worked in an open weave with a silk stiff combination to create a glistening transparent accent that was second to none. Cinderella would have been thrilled to wear this dress when she married her prince. The skirt was delectable, a bit like the Katerina gown's skirt. But the corset, I knew, had to be modern and chic. As a finishing touch, the Swarovski crystal belt that was built onto the exterior of the corset was like a tiara on her waist. With different shapes and sizes, the crystals were like glittering diamonds. Georgia was full of spunk from the time she was a little girl. She wanted to look like a modern-day princess, but not a doll. This dress was going to be all Georgia—with Mom's design aesthetic.

I love bridal, and I'm gratified that so many of my designs were chosen by women for their weddings. Bridal has changed during my lifetime to reflect the brides: women are getting married later in life and sometimes more than once. While the traditional gowns always work, many women want something different, a bit more cutting edge, a bit daring. They want corsets or tuxedos or cocktails dresses or lace or leather. Anything—almost anything—goes, and it makes bridal exciting.

As a non-traditional mother of the bride, I proudly wore the Emmanuelle gown that Giancarlo and I had reworked. Its ethereal and feminine essence was perfection for a July wedding.

I'm lucky in that I know what looks good and what will work when and where. I am a storyteller through fashion. This was my daughter's fairy tale.

The bridal gown featured a specially added loving touch. The bridesmaids would be wearing lilac. Georgia, who's a romantic, wrote her husband-to-be's first name on paper so we could have it embroidered in lilac just as she wrote it, over her heart on the inside of the corset.

Grace made the wedding gown, a true masterpiece. Georgia was ecstatic—my main goal—and she looked like the modern-day princess she wanted to be marrying her prince.

During this entire adventure and honor, I was still carrying on business in my mind. Collection number five was being built months before the wedding gown. My inspiration, the color ways, silhouettes all coming to fruition. This collection was going to be a real statement for the modern woman. The excitement was insurmountable; my team and I were ever so ready to tackle this. FOTINI as a brand was now getting steady traction. We still had a long way to go: the conventional wisdom was that a new designer needs five seasons to show the fashion influencers and powers that be that they are a sustainable business and here to stay. Whether it is your goal is to be picked up by well-known retailers and specialty stores or to attract investors, five seasons was what I was being told by the "strategists."

I was filled with expectations, but sometimes an unexpected turn of events arrives and even our most carefully laid-out plans fade in importance.

CHAPTER TEN
Romanovs and Reality

A girl should be two things: classy and fabulous.
—COCO CHANEL

Most people are well acquainted with the glamour of the fashion industry: the beautifully dressed celebrities, the drama and rhythm of the runway, the magnetism of the individual designers. Not many understand how important less-publicized aspects of the business are: the fabric houses, pattern makers, production leads, your in-house team, and one of the most key people in any design house—the committed salesperson.

For the women who covet and buy the garments, the store where they shop can be the most important aspect. It's certainly true that particular stores can put you on the "map," so to speak. As a designer, especially when you are new in the fashion arena, you rely on the expertise of a seasoned salesperson to introduce you to the right retail real estate opportunities. The salesperson—and their showroom, if applicable—should be your most dedicated cheerleader. This is one of the private faces behind the scenes in fashion. After leaving Fleur

Atelier, I needed a new showroom—with a salesperson who would champion FOTINI—and I needed it soon.

Finding the perfect environment isn't easy, especially when the situation is time sensitive. I was searching for a combination that felt right, that could represent my best interests, to promote the FOTINI brand while being mutually beneficial for both parties.

Ann from my public relations firm recommended the Chiara Fashion Development showroom and arranged for me to meet with Lori, the owner, whom she described as a sharp businesswoman very interested in bringing a luxury brand into her showroom. Chiara did not represent any designer that was at that level and this would help elevate her showroom. We met in a neutral environment to see if we both felt comfortable with one another's goals and vision—time was of the essence for me. There was a mutual need. Lori was a statuesque woman who seemed sharp yet was soft spoken. Could this be the perfect match?

Lori was enthusiastic about the Romanov Collection and assured me that she had great retail connections. She also asked me to bring in pieces from the other collections, an idea I liked as it meant I could show the full range of the FOTINI brand.

"I am going to put you adjacent to another designer whose line is the most upscale brand I currently represent," she said enthusiastically. "You'll complement each other beautifully."

That sounded great to me. I went to the showroom for a tour and found the aesthetic very different from Fleur Atelier's. This was a rawer, loft-style environment with hardwood floors, a minimal space featuring roller rack after roller rack of each designer she represented. Designers had a designated area with signage above their roller racks and within close proximity of each other. I perused the different brands and realized each had its own specialty. The FOTINI brand would really be standing on its own. I had mixed feelings as I finished my walk through, but I had no time to waste with Market Week just around the corner.

Sell, sell, sell! New retail opportunities excited me and fueled my positivity. A surprise awaited me when Lori brought me to where FOTINI would have its home in the showroom. First, I was excited to see that I had a corner with a window featuring natural light to showcase the gems within the collections.

Then my eyes fell upon the space of my neighbor—the designer whose brand would complement FOTINI as FOTINI would hers. The signage above those roller racks, also with a window on the opposite corner, read—Wait, what? Could it be? Gabriela Nowak!

A blast from the past, this was the pushy new designer that Lisa, my first sales representative, who was her friend, had tried to get me to invest in way back. Remember that?

"Oh, I know her." I turned to Lori, my tone neutral, my face expressionless.

"She's fantastic, isn't she?" Lori was excited. "She's my favorite!"

As I looked through the clothes, I was pleasantly surprised to see that Gabriela's line had improved since I'd last seen it; it was more sophisticated, with elevated silhouettes and higher-quality fabrics than in the past. Though the aesthetic remained minimal, the line was more feminine. Yes, she had made me uncomfortable in the past, to say the least, but today, here and now, is a new day. The collection showed talent and possessed a different vision from FOTINI.

I can live with this, I told myself.

The day I brought my Romanov Collection and selected pieces from the previous collections to Chiara, there was Gabriela speaking with Lori. I greeted her enthusiastically and told her how much I liked her designs.

I would make this work. Gabriela and I could live within each other's brand presence. And who knows, we could even complement each other.

I felt better about the arrangement when Lori said, "Gabriela and I think it would be great if you joined us for the Saks Jandel trunk show where she will be, once again, one of the featured designers. This store is perfect for both of your brands."

I had been told about this Washington, DC, boutique by colleagues in the past and how fabulous it was, yet difficult to get into as a new designer. Lori explained, "It's the Beltway's top boutique where dignitaries' wives and socialites shop." This sounded like the chance of a lifetime. *Was it?*

A distant cousin of the Saks Fifth Avenue family had founded this famed retailer. I learned that this legendary store had dressed Nancy Reagan, Barbara Bush, Elizabeth Taylor, and Condoleezza Rice, to name a few. This crowd would embrace FOTINI.

There was no way I would pass up such a great opportunity. And just like that, Vanessa, my loyal assistant, and I were headed to Washington, DC. As an aside, I had heard about the famous cherry blossoms, and they were in full bloom. Into the manicured suburbs, our drive from the airport to our hotel was marked by the scent filling the air with a sweet fragrance and transporting me to a place of beauty and relaxation.

I remembered checking into the minimal and functional hotel Lori had booked us into, thinking that the close proximity to the store was ideal: my focus was on introducing FOTINI and, of course, sales, not on the bells and whistles of fancier hotels.

We all met as a team in the lobby: Vanessa and I, Lori and her business partner, and, of course, Gabriela. We would be walking through the store and meeting staff in preparation for tomorrow, the first day of the trunk show. Off we went. Vanessa and I were very excited about our first time in the legendary store.

When we arrived, I was impressed by the exterior with beautiful window displays featuring more luxury brands than one would dream of. It had an old-world feeling and yet was updated enough without overdoing it—after all, this was a conservative town.

I had expected Saks Jandel to be smaller. Instead I was surprised by the size of the store and the extensive brands it carried: Valentino, Balenciaga, Victoria Beckham, and even my idol, Azzedine Alaïa. The open-concept design made you feel at ease, and I contentedly took my time reviewing the collections. This was going to be one of the best experiences for my brand.

When we left, we headed to dinner as a group with the manager/ head buyer of the store, a woman who had been with Saks Jandel for years and had a record as a great asset. Lori had described her as someone who had superb taste, a good eye, and an in-depth under-standing of the customer—especially the store's rarefied customer. She was known as difficult to impress, so I had my work cut out for me, but I have never steered away from a challenge. Always the best route to go is to be your authentic self.

The restaurant was a beautiful, stately steakhouse, with polished antique wood trim and moldings. Our private dining room contained comfortable chairs and a round table, all in the type of exclusive club feeling that encourages good business dealings. Although somewhat nervous to be meeting this woman who had allowed me to bring my brand to her store, I was pleasantly surprised at how friendly and forthcoming she was with me. Welcoming me to the store and asking questions about my career and family, she was truly interested. In the back of my mind I was once again doing the dance of joy.

I soon noticed that my pleasantries with the buyer were not particularly welcomed by Gabriela. I felt her turn a little chilly in her mannerisms, not engaging in conversation with me all. In fact, she was almost looking right through me. I realized that for Gabriela the competition was on.

As we were about to be seated for dinner, she raced to seat herself by the buyer and she gestured to Lori to sit on the other side. I quickly took it upon myself to take the seat on the buyer's other side instead, with Lori clearly encouraging me to do so to get to know the woman better. On my other side was my trusted Vanessa, then Lori with her business partner. As we continued our conversation, everyone seemed to be having a lovely time, with plenty of both great food and laughter.

It then turned to awkward, followed by uncomfortable.

Gabriela turned the conversation—perhaps for shock value—to an intimate subject between herself and her boyfriend. Although it was relatively short, it felt as if it went on forever.

Thankfully, the evening ended, the dinner having been pleasant overall, and my goal of connecting with this tough-as-nails buyer successfully achieved. When we finally got back to the hotel, I asked Vanessa, "What was *that* all about? Didn't she realize it was embarrassing and not cute?"

Vanessa shrugged. "I think she would have done anything to take the attention away from you, Fotini."

Tomorrow, day one of the trunk show, was going to be interesting.

Morning dawned on a beautiful day, bright and sunny. I awoke with a mix of excitement, butterflies in my stomach, and a dire need for coffee. I went downstairs to the lobby where a continental breakfast was set up for guests. I got my coffee, mixed berries, and yogurt, then rode up in the elevator, hoping all the time I would not bump into *her* before my breakfast.

Dressed in my Sofya navy jacquard dress from the Romanov Collection, I was ready to meet the Capital's famed customers and introduce both FOTINI the brand and Fotini the designer and person.

As a team, led by Lori, we entered the iconic store well before the doors were opened to the public. The manager and her assistant led us to the area where FOTINI and Gabriela Nowak were set up for the next two days. On the right-hand side of the store in the middle was a beautiful area almost like a store-in-store—a salon. This private area had an attractive sofa with two chairs opposite each other and a round glass coffee table topped with fashion industry books and a pretty bouquet of flowers. Before you entered this area, there was a vitrine on the right and on the left. FOTINI was on the left side with a vitrine at my disposal to showcase a look. Then you entered the main salon. On the right was Gabriela's collection with a vitrine for her to display a look. The garments hung beautifully, pressed and ever so strategically placed to show the clients. The night before, prior to our dinner, we had prepared this area, and with the help of the store staff, everything was perfectly set up.

It was now time to take the sales staff through the collections, pointing out the fabrics, construction, and other details important for them to share with clients. It was imperative that they understood this short tutorial, because this would result in what we all wanted—*sales.*

It was now time for the store doors to open, and we were fully ready to impress the Washington, DC, clientele. The understanding was that two models would be showcasing the looks that Gabriela and I had selected, walking around the store so all the clients could see the clothes. There is nothing more appealing than to see the garments on a live body. Every ninety minutes or when told otherwise by Lori, I had been assured, the models would switch from Gabriela's collection to Fotini's and from Fotini's to Gabriela's. That sounded fair, and I expected Lori to be true to her word.

By invitation only, the selected clientele began arriving. Both Vanessa and I soon noted that Lori's focus was primarily on Gabriela's collection. Taking the clients through the garments, Lori and Gabriela were on a mission—weren't we all there for the same reason? Still, since most of these clients were already familiar with Gabriela's brand from past seasons, I was perplexed that Lori wasn't spending any time introducing this new FOTINI brand she claimed to be so proud of.

Patience is a virtue, but everything has its limits. After three hours had passed and the models were still wearing looks from Gabriela's collection, I'd had enough. After all, I had been invited to attend this trunk show. And while I was grateful for that, I hadn't come here to be ignored.

I approached Lori, keeping cool and collected. "What is going on?" I asked. "I thought the schedule was that the models would change every ninety minutes?"

"Oh, we got carried away, but we'll switch midday. Don't worry, Fotini," she said reassuringly.

Midday came and nothing was going to change until I took matters into my own hands. Taking Lori aside, I said sternly, "Have the models change now."

Vanessa and I both realized now that Lori's focus was not going to be on FOTINI. Perhaps she felt I was lucky enough to be there. But let's not forget she was being compensated generously to represent my brand.

I became my own salesperson yet again. I led the customers over to my side of the salon, taking them through the collection, explaining the FOTINI brand and what it stood for. It was also important to me to connect with my customers and understand them. Yes, sales are the goal, but listening and understanding women's needs was my niche. When you sincerely listen and show you are interested in a person, magic happens.

I was dashing in and out of the dressing rooms, pinning hems, altering shoulders on jackets, working on inseams. I found that although I had not yet established a following with this group, they too, like my Houston clientele, wanted and trusted me in the dressing room. And I was so thankful for Vanessa! With the help of that wonderful young woman who often made me laugh in times of chaos, we conquered.

Getting to know these women, interacting with them and hearing about their private lives—something I seemed to bring out in my customers—was one of my true pleasures. I was forewarned by the store manager that a certain VIP and loyal client would be arriving later in the afternoon. At that point, it was pouring rain, so she came in wearing her rain jacket and hat and rubber boots. She immediately told me, "I don't usually look like this," as she took out photographs of her and her husband to show me. Her husband's family was *Social Register* level and had been involved in building one of the most prestigious buildings in Washington. In her early sixties, she was immediately identifiable as an extroverted person who was proud of her good figure and certainly no shrinking violet. The couple were humanitarians and contributors to society. She possessed a couple of my favorite characteristics: straightforward and to the point.

She knew what she wanted and what she was looking for— to wear to an upcoming gala that she and her husband would be hosting. Her eyes fell upon the Calliopi gown. She loved the flattering silhouette, as well as the print and color combination. She did have one firm stipulation: *As long as no one else has it in DC.*

In addition, she wanted the matching Valentina coat with the pleated back and amber-colored Swarovski crystal buttons. I pointed out diplomatically, "The gown and the coat may be a lot of print. Are you comfortable with that?"

With satisfaction and confidence, she was quick to answer, "Oh, yes," knowing she could pull it off.

I was selling and selling plenty from the collections! Another lovely woman purchased the Fedora cocktail dress for her upcoming wedding. I was thrilled to be gaining these new clients and making such a solid impact in my first time at this important store. With day two coming, I was determined that I would show up with the same attitude. You are your own salesperson and no one can connect with the client better than you.

As the day ended I was mentally and physically exhausted, as well as very upset with my "supposed" salesperson.

In my room at the hotel, I reviewed the day in my head. I had been run off my feet with no help. The salespeople from the store couldn't cater only to the featured designers—they had to serve the entire store. Listening and hearing the needs of these lovely women was wonderful, but it was also a lot to process mentally, especially when meeting them for the first time. I never took anything for granted and, as grueling the day had been, I knew I was extremely fortunate to be starting to build loyalty and a relationship with these women.

Day one of the trunk show was a success, and I was going to make sure day two was as well. Still the dark cloud weighed on my mind; I had been sharply let down by someone I was paying to help me going forward in the sales of my brand. That someone had reassured me that she was on my side and would support me "as family," that she would be my cheerleader.

When Lori suggested dinner that evening at a casual local restaurant—to include Gabriela—I reluctantly agreed. I was pleased that Gabriela showed up only for a drink and didn't stay to dine. Perhaps it was for the best, because I was given the cold shoulder even on the rare moments I had tried to converse with her throughout the day, much like the dinner the night before. I wasn't sure she took the success of my day one was taken too well.

At the cozy patio bar set far back in the restaurant, I sat in the midst of greenery taking in the fresh spring air. The rain had stopped, the sun had returned to shining ever so brightly. The scent of the blossoms was invigorating yet calming. This seemed like a good place to broach a difficult subject.

We were ready to relax and enjoy a cold glass of white wine when Lori, in a friendly manner, expressed how pleased she was with the successful FOTINI sales.

It was like a lightning bolt hit me. I expressed my disappointment and bluntly, if politely, told her that tomorrow on day two, I expected her to fulfill her role as my salesperson and spend time on FOTINI. "The customer already knows Gabriela. I need the support. I am only one person, Lori."

She assured me day two would be focused on FOTINI. I can't say I had much faith at that point, but I always hoped for the best. I had survived four seasons in this intense industry, after jumping into the lion's den. To my advantage, I had come to the fashion world as a seasoned business professional and was definitely not naïve (*Thank you, Dad!*).

My instincts have always led me, and I listen carefully. A wise mentor once told me "Always ask yourself in your heart of hearts what do you really believe," and in this case with Lori and Chiara, I did know what the final outcome would be. I continued to stay focused.

Compromises in life and business have to be made, especially when you are entering a new industry, when you are an entrepreneur. You have to earn your way, as I learned at a very young age. You have to do the time and put in those hours, and then you appreciate your success even more.

For example, when a customer mentioned at a past trunk show that I should be charging twice what I did for the quality, craftsmanship, and care that FOTINI represented as a brand, I knew she was right. But compromises and sacrifices are part of the process to build the success of your business.

The wool had not been pulled over my eyes by any means. By now I had a grasp on how to navigate this industry to some degree—I was not the new kid on the block, so to speak. I began to realize that it was time to make some serious decisions and also draw firm lines. Always be aware of your surroundings and the people in them.

Day two had come, another great sunny day and a very warm one. My wardrobe choice was from the Wisteria Collection, a beautiful pink silk chiffon printed, button-down dress with an elbow-length sleeve and a waistline accented by a thin, pink belt.

As we approached the store and the doors opened for us, I was exhilarated!

There at the entrance of the store stood this magnificent mannequin wearing none other than the exquisite Katerina gown from the Romanov collection in all her glory. Who wouldn't be impressed to be greeted by the sight of the layered skirt of morel-colored silk tulle, the floral velvet belt at the waist, and the sculpted corset showcasing the jacquard overlay?

My eyes welled up with tears and pride—I was grateful and thrilled.

Not everyone was.

Gabriela walked right by the display, and, quite frankly, I couldn't have cared less. We didn't need to be friends to coexist in a showroom or share time at a trunk show. Lori spent a short time with me while clients came in, and I realized what was probably one of the key reasons we couldn't work together: she didn't have a clue how to sell FOTINI. I watched her describe the garments to some of the clients, and she could not do them justice. You would think that since she was representing this brand and after extensive conversations about the details of FOTINI, she would be well versed when describing the garments to the clients. But she really was out of her realm with this luxury brand. If you don't believe in the product you are selling, how can you successfully sell to the customer? The writing was on the wall.

Let me backtrack a little to the car ride to the store that morning. We drove to the store together, all five of us—Lori driving, Gabriela in the passenger seat, and Lori's business partner, Vanessa, and I in the back seat. It became clear that Lori had spoken to Gabriela about my concerns around the lack of attention she was giving FOTINI when Gabriela started putting down a past designer Lori had represented, a celebrity favorite and winner of a famed design competition.

"Remember how much attention he demanded at one of the trunk shows, Lori? What an awful crybaby he was, whining that you weren't paying attention to him? Remember the tantrums?"

Vanessa and I exchanged a look. We were obviously supposed to know that I was being compared to a "crybaby."

Receiving attention from Chiara was what I was paying Lori for. What was I missing here?

From when I first met Gabriela through Lisa and their underhanded ways to get me to invest, I was well acquainted with her conniving behavior. Now, after spending time with her, I did not expect maturity, manners, professionalism, or class from her, and didn't care what she thought or said. It was Lori who had disappointed me yet again, Lori who had betrayed my confidences and discussed my concerns with Gabriela. I now knew where her loyalties lay.

Day two at Saks Jandel was a great success! I was prepared for the running around and ready to be my own salesperson. I sold not only from the Romanov Collection, but also from the past collections more than once. I'd had three requests for the Calliopi gown that I had given my word not to sell again in the entire DC area. I turned those requests into other sales: the Raina cocktail dress, the Vera leather top and pencil skirt (a big seller as a suit). The Elena jacquard suit was a big hit, and one of the all-time favorites was the Natalia leather dress with the exposed zipper, showing that this crowd was both conservative and chic.

When the day concluded and we were tallying up our sales, Lori pleasantly said, "Fantastic job, Fotini."

"Yes, thank you," I replied proudly. "Aren't I a great salesperson?" I got a nod and a little smile from her.

Perhaps the hardest part about traveling to trunk shows is that there really is no down time from the pressure. Fitness is a big part of my life and I always tried to get a run in at the start of the day, but that didn't necessarily happen. Albeit not part of a fitness regime, Vanessa and I did manage to go to the Jimmy Choo store on a whim, because I had forgotten my flats. We both came out with some shoe candy!

This trip had me thinking more than ever about my next steps for the business. Back in New York, during Market Week, Sara from Houston came to look at the Romanov Collection and to buy for her store. This was her first time visiting me at the Chiara showroom. As always, she was honest and a breath of fresh air, so it came as no surprise when she asked me point-blank, "What on earth are you doing in this showroom? This is not going to elevate your brand, Fotini. You can do better than this!"

I knew that very well by now.

There was no way I would be back at Chiara after this season, but since we had an agreement, I wanted to make the best of Lori's retail connections. I was elated when she approached me about a store in the Middle East that was interested in the line. Lori had sent my look book and said they'd fallen in love with the richness of the Romanov Collection. "They adore over-the-top luxury," she stated.

I was pleased. "That sounds promising."

"They've already placed an order." She handed me a spreadsheet. "Here are the pieces."

I immediately spoke to Juliet, who would be in charge of production. "We have this new order," I told her happily. "We have a lot of production and I want to make sure we can deliver."

She responded with, "We can do this, Fotini," and if I trusted anyone, it was this wonderful woman.

As a team, we had sat down upon my return from DC and discussed the trunk show and the events around it. Everyone was disappointed at Chiara's performance and pointed out that this may not have been a match made in heaven. Juliet knew someone she trusted who currently worked at the famed designer's studio—the designer Gabriela had referred to as "the crybaby" Lori used to represent. Juliet said she would speak to her acquaintance to get feedback from the designer about the showroom.

Without mentioning my name, she did just that, and the report she came back with wasn't encouraging. This designer's message was that Lori had given his brand no attention and that he had done all the selling himself. How familiar that sounded!

Then there were the "phantom orders" that followed.

The message to me from him was, "Tell that designer to run away from there as fast as she can."

Yes, the "phantom orders." The Middle East order turned out to be one of those. We produced the order, but it never shipped. A surprising cancellation with unsold inventory. What had happened? A retailer showing interest in a collection does not translate into a solid order or even the hope that it will turn into one. Only a signed order is a real order! Due to Lori, we had also put in a large stock order for other opportunities that never came through. Needless to say, all this inventory cost a lot of money to produce.

Juliet had had enough. This was a woman who cared about me and the FOTINI brand as if it were her own. She believed in it and was proud of what it stood for.

"You need to think about what your next move is in regards to sales," she said caringly and honestly. "I think that means a dedicated salesperson—dedicated to FOTINI alone."

My heart swelled at her support and loyalty. And I knew she was right. This woman was a seasoned professional in this industry and had seen it all. Going into this next season, the fifth, was pivotal. The brand was clearly being well received and had earned respect to where I was working with the most reputable groups in the Garment District. There was traction. What I needed more than ever was someone to sell and take the brand to the right retail opportunities and doors.

This would be a big investment and one of the most important ones in my fashion career. I was tired of the posers, the big talkers and their hangers-on, those who overpromised and underdelivered. I felt strongly and fully prepared to make the hard choices. It was time.

Simultaneously, MediaMode was handling my public relations presence and I carefully attended the events they selected for me. I was not interested in being at every social event in Manhattan. That is not me. But I would attend anything that was beneficial to the brand.

One event I went to was the 100 Years Celebration of the Gordon Parks Foundation, hosted by Tommy Hilfiger at the legendary Plaza Hotel, recognizing honorees in the name of the great photographer and humanitarian, Gordon Parks. I had purchased seats and attended with a well-respected businesswoman and socialite who wore the Lola cocktail dress with Chantilly lace and organza from the Javiera Collection, while I had chosen the Jolie cocktail dress with embroidered tulle and organza from the Wisteria Collection. I met several icons, including Bernadette Peters, a favorite with whom I had a lovely chat, the gorgeous Lauren Hutton, and designer Alexander Wang. Sitting at the table behind us was Sofia Vergara, even more beautiful in person. I spoke briefly to her before she was whisked away by her then fiancé. I wanted to tell her that we shared a bust form at the same atelier—but of course I wasn't going to do that.

These events are another part of the responsibilities of having a fashion business. Some are a lot of fun, but often enough they are not. Still, it's always important to make oneself visible at these platforms and, of course, to meet people and network. It was the perfect thing to cleanse my palate of the bad taste the past few weeks had left behind.

There are many bright spots in the industry, and what could be more rewarding than making your fairy tale come true, even if it includes an ogre or two?

I am fortunate in that I have the ability to shrug off unpleasantness and stay focused. There are many bright spots in the industry, and what could be more rewarding than making your fairy tale come true, even if it includes an ogre or two?

Life is very much like designing a collection. My process always begins with inspirations that come from personal experiences in my childhood and adulthood, through travel, art, and movies. I visualize the entire picture—fabric choices, colors, the details of the lace, the motif of the beading—always with a mood board, on which to clip and paste images that would be relevant to the collection. This is a wonderful way to play around with different ideas. Research formed a large part of my approach to each season for FOTINI, helping me understand what I wanted to communicate to my audience, and how to make it interesting yet not foreign so that they do not misunderstand my message.

Similarly, in life we have dreams, perhaps inspired by a person, an industry, a visionary, or someone in our own family. We can plan our first step through education or go and experience real hands-on work or maybe do both: Life has to happen and you have to let it. For most of us, our careers evolve organically. We don't necessarily end up in the same business that we set out to build. That isn't even the goal, and there may be other opportunities that you haven't thought of. My goal has always been to end positively and allow ideas to keep evolving into doing what I truly love. If you're not evolving, you are not growing and you stop learning.

Design for me is a process of vision, inspiration, and research. It's discipline, work, and perseverance that make dreams come true.

When I was in Italy learning the stitching of corsetry, I reminded myself that life is like stitching. Although creating a corset was sometimes difficult and my fingers hurt from the stitching, *every stitch* built the garment and achieved the final goal.

Trying not to let the naysayers get the best of me was a challenge that was sometimes very difficult in this very lonely industry. In the long run, those people were not the ones who mattered. The ones who mattered would always be the women I designed for. I created and produced special pieces in my collections because that was what they came to expect from my niche brand and me. I wanted my customers to feel special. Like my favorite crayons as a child, they were my metallic shades.

That is why my trunk shows at Saks Jandel and other stores were so rewarding in spite of the stress. To have emotional fulfilment, work can never be just about sales. For me, it was about the feedback I got that women felt special in my creations. The customers and audience must always be treated well, like metallic crayons. I appreciated their loyalty and returned it, and I tried to exceed their expectations.

I use the word "authentic" as many do today, and I don't take this lightly. For me, it is a vital characteristic, one that I value in myself and in others, one that leads to trust and success. Even as a little girl designing for my dolls, my goal was to make them look beautiful, their best.

I listened carefully to my customers, heard what they had to say, how they wanted to represent themselves. Through this, my mantra was always "The customer first."

I want to enhance you. I don't want to change you.

To further my reach to more women meant I was going to have to find a solid and well-connected sales representative. This is the key for any designer. Not just a tough sales representative, not just a hustler, but also someone who genuinely believes in the brand overall—who understands it and appreciates how special it is.

That is why I told Juliet to start the search by asking around through her connections, as I would do the same. Being in the industry for as long as she had, Juliet's reach was much more extensive than mine and she had an innate ability to know what would work.

Meanwhile, the mood boards for collection number five were exploding. My inspiration came from my childhood this time.

Nothing could get my team and me down now—we were all so inspired and excited. My vision was of empowerment of women: a tribute celebrating strength, power, independence, and femininity without frills, dedicated to women who spoke their minds and had something to say even without saying it.

The fifth collection was on its way. And it was going to be the best one yet!

CHAPTER ELEVEN
Binding the Seams

Some things evolve as they should without
our knowing it. Just let them.
—FOTINI

O n a gray and rainy Sunday, a day that called for staying home curled up with a good book or watching movies, I did the opposite. I told myself that my routine and errands must be met—part of my self-discipline, I suppose. I began by going to the gym that morning, followed by a trip to Bed Bath & Beyond for studio supplies, and finally a visit to the Whole Foods at Columbus Circle, convenient to my apartment and a usual end-of-day stop for groceries.

I walked home in the drizzle, deciding that a relaxing movie and Sunday dinner were ahead of me for the evening. I would curl up with a glass of wine, my biggest decision being the selection of a film. Tomorrow, I would deal with the ongoing emotions that had been lightly rumbling in my head like distant thunder—I ordered myself to enjoy the rest of the day.

I'd just gotten home when the phone rang, wondering who would be calling on a Sunday afternoon. When I saw the telephone number of my Toronto home on the call display, I figured it was my husband wanting to chat, a welcomed afternoon treat. So I thought.

It turned out not to be a welcome call at all: I froze at the news that my husband was being rushed to the emergency room. I was being told to calm down, that everything was under control, but I was sure it wasn't. I felt it. So many emotions started flooding through my entire body. First came the crying. On the heels of that came panic, as I questioned whether or not I was getting the full story, how this had happened. The list went on and on. Being the person I am, I am typically the leader, organizer, nurturer, the one in control of ensuring that everyone else is okay and looked after.

Some things in life are out of our hands. One cannot always be the captain of the ship, a loss of control I don't relate to well at all.

My first impulse was to rush to the airport and hop on a flight to Toronto. I was completely devastated and terribly afraid. I'm happy to say that Georgia and her soon-to-be husband, Lucas, hurried to the hospital to see what was really going on. If anyone was going to get the facts on my behalf, it was Georgia. Not everyone was happy with this, but she was one of my first mates. She was given a mission by me, and she was going to get results.

An hour or two later, I finally had the opportunity to speak to my husband in the hospital ER. He was adamant that flying home was not necessary. I had key buyers from very important retailers coming in the following day, and he did not want me to miss that appointment as another with them wouldn't be easily secured. He reassured me as many times as he could that everything was moving along and promised to tell me if I needed to book a flight. Soon afterward, Georgia relayed all the information she could discover about what was going on—both the good and bad details she thought I needed to know, the details my reassuring husband had left out. My first mates—I can count on them forever!

This incident left me disoriented. It was not easily compartmentalized. I had no idea how to feel or what to feel. That evening when I went to bed, I barely slept. The illness of my husband and the ongoing health issues that had led to the hospital, the upcoming nuptials of my daughter, and the demands of the exacting business I had built in this challenging yet wonderful city were all swirling around in my mind.

Soldier on, Fotini! I ordered. *Now is not the time to stop leading the many ships you are steering. Everyone needs you.*

Over the next couple of days, everything calmed down somewhat. My husband was doing better and at home now, and I had successfully handled my meeting with the retailers. I was going to Toronto that following weekend to fulfill my mother of the bride duties: assisting in the wedding preparations and tastings and finalizing my daughter's bridal shower details. I was still working on Georgia's wedding gown with Grace Tsui.

On Friday, I packed the last-minute items for my trip to Canada. It was a gorgeous New York morning, with bright skies and cotton candy clouds—from the twenty-sixth floor, it was like looking at a postcard. My feelings didn't match the calm placidity of the view, though. As I stood in my kitchen sipping caramel-flavored coffee and looking out the window, a wave of fear and unsettledness came over me. *I need to be here in New York, in order to drive this business to the next level,* I thought. The 75 percent of my time that I spent in this city was no longer enough. There were options like those some designers chose, for example, they remained in their home cities, their bases, and had their teams run the business in New York. I knew of a few instances like this where the designer would fly in two to three times a month to review samples and prototypes then fly back. I never considered this an alternative. In fact, it was a key discussion point between my husband and me before I started this business—and we both fully agreed.

As I said, I was the captain of this ship and my team needed me at the helm, leading, motivating, and creating. As when I was a little girl seated on the veranda of my home coloring or creating a pattern on my Spirograph, I was the driving force of the vision. As when I was in my nursery school and the teacher had set up an easel and paints for me in a corner away from the children who bullied me, I was in charge of my personal ship. I was not about to let go.

As the plane lifted into the sky bound for Toronto, I had a gut-wrenching pain in my stomach and tears in my eyes. Something did not feel right.

Keep it together. Now is the time to be happy for your little girl, I told myself sternly. *Your concerns will have to wait.*

I went into full "mother of the bride" mode, and it was one of the best times of my life. Georgia's bridal shower was beautiful, and although I hosted, it was always with her in mind. It was her time. For some reason, Georgia always seemed to have the perfect weather. This, too, was a beautiful day spent with family that included many friends, as well as grandmothers who were over the moon they could attend. And I, too, received a gift: the smile on my daughter's face the entire time.

I spent a week in Toronto and was very happy to see that my husband was back to his normal busy schedule. That gave me peace and comfort, which was made even greater by being with my little Bronx, whom I missed more than ever when he was here rather than with me every day in New York.

Calls with my team took place daily: looking at the patterns and samples on the fit model, reviewing the fabrics that had come in, and having to deal with how frustrating it was to not be there to see certain details. Perhaps it is just who I am, but I need to feel and touch to see things in real time and in person.

After the tastings and final details for the wedding, it was time to head back to New York. Quite frankly, I was more than ready to get back. Still, as my plane was descending into Newark, that wave of fear swept over me again.

Why was I feeling like this?

From Newark to my apartment on the Upper West Side, it was a thirty-five minute ride with no traffic. The car was heading into the city and as I was approaching home from afar, I could see the Hearst Tower, which meant I was almost there. At that moment I was very happy to be back, eager to tackle collection five and its beauty!

Off to the studio!

At 336 West 37th Street, I got off on the fourteenth floor as usual. I was about to enter the studio when I saw the white sign on the door, with the FOTINI logo in silver, staring back at me in an intense yet profound way.

The sick feeling in my stomach was back with a vengeance and so were the tears. I was impatient, asking myself, *How long will this last?* From the beginning, this question had been relentless.

I quickly pushed open the door, not allowing those emotions to overtake me. Vanessa, Juliet, and her assistant, Isabel, were at their usual places at the table, while Gino sat behind her in his own space working his magic. On the pattern table were the gorgeous rolls of fabrics that had come in while I was in Toronto. Of course, staring at me were my fifth collection mood boards, covered with inspiration images and fabrics, colors, and various other swatches I'd selected. This was one of my favorite parts of the design process.

"I'm baaack," I said joyfully, smiling at their wonderful faces. Not for a moment were they going to see or feel my dark clouds.

The gratitude filling me at that moment was immeasurable: this amazing group I had pulled together to be my team were so obviously happy to see me. I felt that especially from Gino, as I did upon my return from every trip I took to Canada. In the blink of an eye, we were all back to business. I went home that night feeling content and happy to be back. Looking out my windows at the lights of the city I loved, I told myself, *You've got this, Fotini. Just keep calm and carry on!*

The preparations for Georgia's wedding were coming fast and furious now, and we were all caught up in the excitement. Two weeks after my return, my daughter flew in for her second bridal gown fitting, arriving at the studio blazing brightness and warmth like a fireball. Everyone at FOTINI was very excited to see this little lady with the huge personality again, including Grace Tsui, who was on hand with the gown in its initial stages. When Georgia stepped into the skirt with its layers upon layers of silk tulle and the pinned corset, we all gasped. Grace had managed to capture everything we wanted in this fairy-tale gown and more—and it wasn't even finished yet. We made some changes and Grace was then on her way.

"Curious Georgia" was looking at all the sketches on the wall showing the silhouettes I'd approved for the upcoming collection and the swatches for each look.

She carefully scanned everything before saying, "Mom, these are beautiful. I'm so proud of what you have accomplished! I know how hard you have been working, but it's all worth it."

As if on cue, there came that pain in my stomach again.

We enjoyed the couple of days she was in town, going to dinner in the evenings, catching up, talking about the coming wedding. We had a lot of fun. And then she was off to the airport.

Georgia's leaving was hard for me, but her visit and her pride in my work had made my heart sing. It brought to mind the time my youngest daughter, Calli, had flown in during the early stages of the FOTINI brand, meeting my team and soaking in what this business was—from the mood boards to the fabric table, seeing my hard work and the fruit it bore, as well. One of my favorite memories was our going out several nights in a row, in spite of pouring rain, to dine at the downtown Cipriani because Calli loved their Bolognese. No downpour was going to stop us!

I was so proud of my two girls.

The collection had been moving along on schedule. At the same time, I was interviewing salespeople with Juliet. Everything should have been well and good, yet I was starting to lose sleep and unable to shake my feeling of uneasiness. The bouts were lasting longer and kept coming more frequently. This doom and gloom had to stop, but would it?

I thought back upon my lifetime thus far. From the tiny girl on an airplane headed to Greece on her own and wondering why she wasn't with her family, to the teenager who thought her life was ruined because of having to wear a back brace, I had been making sacrifices for the end goal without even knowing it.

What, I wondered, *what is the goal in this chapter of FOTINI?*

Suddenly, it was wedding time. On this trip, I personally carried my daughter's wedding gown through LaGuardia Airport, never my favorite place. Nothing was going to threaten the delivery of this masterpiece on my watch!

Saturday, July 6, 2013, arrived.

Again, Georgia managed to have somehow worked with the weather gods and the day was perfection, gloriously sunny with the temperature in the eighties. The Fallsview Casino in Niagara Falls, Canada, was equally perfect. As the falls cascaded down, my little girl prepared to get married. The preparations were filled with laughter and joy, as Georgia's bridesmaids and the bridal party were getting our hair and makeup done by the glam squad we had booked.

When the time came to help the bride into her princess gown, I was in charge. As I secured every hook and eye, made sure the bow in the back sat in its perfect position, fluffed the tulle, and tied the corset, I felt both pride and sadness. This was it! Although she had been living with Lucas for a few years now, my darling daughter would soon officially be someone's wife and partner, not just my little girl anymore.

As she turned around, the entire room of bridesmaids and family started to cry tears of joy. Georgia was absolutely gorgeous, beaming with happiness and making sure we all knew it was her day. From the time she was a baby, Georgia has always been a comedian of sorts, and with her exaggerated manner, she always managed to ensure everyone understood her intentions.

It was then my turn to get ready. I rushed to my room and put on another gorgeous FOTINI creation—the Emmanuelle gown. I could not have been prouder.

And so it began.

As her father and I walked Georgia down the aisle, the look on her face was one of pure joy. At the altar, Lucas not only looked the handsomest I'd ever seen him, but the way he looked at the woman becoming his wife (and the way she gazed back) was like a magnet and steel: I felt their bond. As my eyes went to my youngest daughter, Calli, standing with the rest of the bridesmaids, I was moved by how beautiful these two young women were, my little girls. The wedding party also included little Bronx and Kimbo, Georgia's puppy, the two attracting more attention than ever as they trotted down the aisle, a sweet touch.

We danced, ate, and were merry. I managed to keep myself together and not blubber away during my speech, although I did find myself a couple of times unable to look directly at this young married woman of whom I was speaking. And, just like that, the fairy tale ended with a happily ever after.

I'd be back to reality and dealing with that gut-wrenching pain once and for all soon enough.

During the festivities and excitement of this wonderful life moment, I chose to do nothing but stay focused on my family. Standing behind the scenes and looking through what felt like a mirror, I watched carefully what was in front of me. My husband's health concerns were my concerns as well. We had several discussions around this and how life was going to work with me being in New York and the pressing demands of the business. That weighed on my mind more than anything else, and I was going to have to carefully think about the long term.

Without many words being said or unsaid, I faced my worst career fear—the question that the white and silver FOTINI sign on my studio door kept asking me: "How long will this last?"

Where did my brand fit into my life now?

Throughout the wonderful experience of studying design with brilliant artisans and having my own fashion house, all the while I was fulfilling my dream over the last few years, what I was realizing is that the most gratifying part of it all was the clients wearing my creations. This had taken a gradual and unexpected turn to the point where I was now advising them about their overall personal brand. In addition to their clothing, I was discussing the aesthetic of their interiors and the fabrics to be used, reviewing paint colors for their walls. I was helping them develop the themes of life events such as weddings from fashion to floral arrangements. And, more and more, I was consulting on how to rebrand themselves to achieve career goals. This is something I was sought out for, something I had been doing by request for friends even before my business started. This was so natural and organic.

But now back to the most pressing matter: my upcoming fifth collection—the most powerful one yet!

Flying through the clouds on my way back to New York after the wedding with all these thoughts running through my mind, I felt as if I didn't want the plane to land. My concerns over the future of FOTINI had been creeping up and were always with me, no matter where I went. Although I knew what had to be said and done, it felt wrong. I was sad, feeling that I was being forced to do what I felt was wrong and yet was right in every way. With tears streaming down my face and feeling sick to my stomach, I looked out the window wondering how to get through this.

How could I abandon all I had ever wanted, especially at this time when everything was starting to fall into place? What about my team, the team I considered my extended family? As we were descending into Newark, I would not take my eyes away from the window while I wiped my tears and collected myself, thankful no one was seated beside me. What I felt, I knew, was grief for the loss that lay ahead.

On the ground, I stuck to my usual routine, going to the apartment to drop off my bag then hurrying to the studio. Facing the FOTINI sign on my studio door that day was one of the hardest things I have had to do. With a smile, I entered to see my team sitting at the main table waiting for me. More fabrics had arrived, the colors vibrant, the metallic accents gleaming.

I spoke privately with each of them, being as honest and open as I had always been. I first talked to Vanessa, explaining the challenge of family obligations and what going forward would mean for me. I explained that I had to make a very difficult and life-changing decision at this time. Fashion or family. I had already decided.

Vanessa couldn't believe what she was hearing. This young woman knew me perhaps better than any other team

Fashion or family. I had already decided.

member. She sat at the head of the table in our studio because most of the time she was in charge—of me! Time and again she had seen how devoted and committed I was to the business, often saying, "I don't know how you do it." From traveling with me to understanding how alone I was, she knew me well and called me a role model. I know I influenced this woman in many ways both personally and professionally. After all we'd gone through together, she was like another daughter to me. She was my confidante and always managed to make me laugh. I knew she would be fine—she was bright and had grown to a level where she was managing me and the day-to-day business, all the while supporting the whole team.

Gino was more of a concern for me as to how he would take the news. He'd become my friend and creative counterpart. The laughs we would have were really something. I remembered laughing so hard once over his imitation of Salma Hayek's magazine spread in *InStyle*—we both loved her and adored the drama of the photo shoot, her extravagant gowns and her facial expressions. I thought about our shared love of some celebrities like Victoria Beckham and Dita Von Teese. Our visits to retailers reviewing collections and sometimes questioning the designer's inspirations were a special bond. I knew this was going to hit him hard, and it did. There were tears in his eyes, the tears of abandonment. I explained the circumstances and the difficulty around my decision. We were all invested in this brand and even more excited than ever before because of the opportunities we had ahead of us. I could feel his sense of loss. I had always treated him like a true equal—creatively and financially—and the opportunity of being part of this brand and its growth was very important to him.

I then met with Juliet who, in her true "Juliet class" way, understood in spite of her deep sadness. "What does this mean, Fotini?" she asked in her most comforting voice. She was determined to keep the brand going, and I felt and respected her loyalty.

I was not sure what it meant myself. How could I articulate it best to this woman, whom I respected at the utmost level?

"What does this mean, Fotini?" It was everyone's question: Grace, Giancarlo, production houses, embroidery and fabric suppliers, my PR firm. It left so many people shocked and wondering what was coming next. The only thing I knew for sure was that there is a "pause" button in life that can be pressed.

The next couple of weeks, we gathered as a team and soldiered on. We found a fabric buyer who was interested in the fabrics I chose to sell while the rest were put in storage. As it turned out, my studio space and Betsey Johnson's were being taken over by an existing tenant who was expanding. My landlord asked if I wanted a space he had secured for me on the ninth floor, larger and quite lovely. He respected me for being a star tenant who paid on time and he valued my professionalism. In the fashion industry, paying on time counts for a lot.

Every part of me wanted to say, "Yes, yes, yes! I will take the space," but I knew at this time it was not going to happen. I also spoke with the landlord of my apartment and gave him the appropriate notice, and he, too, was saddened, telling me, "You are a lovely woman and the best tenant I've ever had." I knew that the apartment would be taken in a nanosecond and, sure enough, within forty-eight hours, apartment 26S was off the market.

My good friend Christina, the woman who had brought me my brilliant stylist, Allison, and her partner came to look at some of my furniture for their new place and I was very happy to offer her what she could use. She had been one of my true friends in New York, someone I could trust, someone I admired and respected professionally, and someone I hold close to my heart to this day. When I had told her the news, she understood. Like Vanessa, and even before Vanessa had come into my life, she had walked through the fires with me.

I've always loved photography, especially portraits, which I think make charming wall accents. As I was taking down the framed photographs of Madonna, Marilyn Monroe, Brad Pitt, Richard Gere, and Eva Mendes, I found a sense of calm, sadness, and reality. This was really happening. I kept only those pieces that genuinely meant something to me, selling everything else in the apartment.

One warm evening, I did what I always needed to do to clear my head and bring clarity. A run through my beloved Central Park just a few blocks away was in order.

I was sweating fiercely as I raced along. I looked at the sky, the people, the statues, and felt almost as if I were going through a cleanse. I ended in Strawberry Fields, the memorial area for John Lennon, staring down at the Imagine mosaic.

I did just that—I imagined what the next chapter would look like. Isn't that what vision is? Isn't that what dreams are built on? This was my next chapter and I had to hold on to some of my character traits: my perseverance, drive, and determination. When I went home after that run and showered, what felt like the biggest weight was not gone but felt lighter. My staff would be all right; they had their next steps already in motion, and, with their talents, I knew it wouldn't be long before they were settled. Of course, they all wanted me to keep them informed of my next steps with the FOTINI label, and I promised I would do that.

I knew that now the hardest part for me would be closing the studio door for the last time. One last time in that space, on that floor, in Suite 1450. Reluctantly, yet at peace with my decision, I opened the front door and found myself in an almost empty space with just a few items left that Vanessa had been looking after for me. I was brought back to the day my friend, Terry, and I started to set up the studio: the uncertainty, the excitement, the unknown. When I stepped out onto the balcony where Bronx would come out and sniff the air, I looked at the distant view of the water and the view just across to Giancarlo's studio, and the tears began. What a wonderful time I had spent here!

When I walked back in, I touched the walls for the last time. I sat on the floor with a glass of wine from the last bottle in the otherwise empty fridge. I toasted Fotini the person, FOTINI the brand, and all that had been accomplished. I was, and am, really proud of myself and excited about what is yet to come.

I got up, put the wineglass in the corner with the bottle beside it, picked up the bag of odds and ends Vanessa had put aside for me, and walked to the door. Turning around, I took a final look around the room, remembering the laughter, the challenging times, and the faces that would be forever embedded in my mind. The bottle of wine sitting in the corner—*unfinished*—caught my eye, and I thought, *Like my story.*

I turned and walked out, closing the door behind me and locking it. When I took down the white and silver FOTINI sign, I held it close to me, no longer asking, *How long will this last?*

Now I asked, *Where will I hang you next?*

In August of 2013, I was back in Toronto still reeling from all these emotions and taking some time to adjust to a more consistent schedule. Gary Roth, our trusted accountant, called from New York. A colorful, stylish, and bright man, Gary has long worked with some of the most notable players in the fashion industry. Both my husband and I respected his integrity and support for FOTINI—he was a true cheerleader and knew how hard I'd worked, not only on the designs but also on building the brand. He told me now how much he respected and admired me and the gorgeous collections I produced, and how he was looking forward to the next one. In his matter-of-fact voice, he also said he understood my reasons for pushing the pause button.

He next said he had an important question he felt he had to ask. "Aside from not having a dedicated and professional salesperson, why was FOTINI not yet in a major retailer?

I thought David Randall was going to be the driving force in making that happen, especially with Bergdorf Goodman and all his connections there," he noted. He went on to say that he felt as strongly as we all did that this brand belonged in the legendary store, that the craftsmanship, tailoring, and overall aesthetic of FOTINI perfectly fit Bergdorf Goodman and the store's target demographic.

"After earning your way and proving this is a luxury brand, what happened to David's support?"

Gary wanted to get to the bottom of this unanswered question and, since David's DRA was one of his clients, he decided to ask. When we received a call back from him, we heard anger and frustration in Gary's usual matter-of-fact tone.

He explained that, unbeknownst to any of us, David *had* been offered an opportunity to get the FOTINI brand into Bergdorf Goodman. That is, he had been given a chance to get *one of his designers* in. Unfortunately for me, the other designer was an extremely well-connected, well-known New Yorker. David chose the other designer for reasons that don't even have to be said. Gary was sincerely outraged and disgusted. I felt betrayed, but I was also happy to finally be free of the clutches of so many of these "supporters" who assured us they believed in FOTINI.

Some very happy news had come to me before I closed the studio: Allison was engaged. I was ecstatic for my wonderful friend. I treasured our relationship and all we had shared while I was in New York. When we sat down in my studio, and I proceeded to tell her the news, I could see she was sad, and yet she was sympathetic and reassuring because she knew and understood my family challenges. She had, in a caring and respectful way, brought up the possibility of my designing her wedding gown, mentioning it without any pressure during this difficult time. It had devastated me to say that, because of the timing, I couldn't commit to producing what would have been a masterpiece. This woman was and is beautiful inside and out, and I would have been so very proud to design her gown. But I never take anything on unless I know I can give one hundred percent, which would have been impossible.

What I could commit to was making her a custom suit for the day-after-the-wedding brunch. I made her the Madelaine jacket and Angelique dress from the Wisteria Collection, in white corded cotton.

I was so happy and honored to be at her beautiful California wedding. Sharing in her "happily ever after" moment gave me such pleasure and she looked magnificent! The wedding was covered by the *New York Times* and *Martha Stewart Weddings,* and it was a magical day for everyone present.

What did I learn and take away from my time in New York? I learned the importance of perseverance and the fact that hard work will pay off. There are no short cuts. You have to put in the time and earn your way. Understanding how to run a business is a skill that includes understanding what is important and what is not before anything else in order to achieve sustainability. I left New York strengthened in my beliefs that it doesn't cost anything to be kind and that honesty and integrity are the keys to sleeping at night. There are bad apples everywhere you go, but you must never lose faith that people are good. It is vital to remain true to your vision and focus: don't be stubborn, stay open-minded, but don't let anyone steer you outside your lane if it doesn't feel authentic. I now have some friends and great people that will be in my life forever.

I know that I helped others grow during that period. It was, and will always remain, my goal in business as in life.

I know that I helped others grow during that period. It was, and will always remain, my goal in business as in life.

- My contribution as a business owner, one who supported her suppliers by being honest and respectful.

- The knowledge that I gave my clients along with the beautifully crafted garments fashioned out of extraordinary fabrics.

- My willingness to always listen carefully to what the clients wanted and needed and give them my professional advice to bring out the best of themselves through fashion and lifestyle.

- My mentorship of my staff—perhaps my most valuable contribution, and one in which I take great pride.

My main takeaway is that I know that the little girl on the

veranda fulfilled her dream and has what it takes to survive the fashion industry and whatever else lies in her career path. That Ms. Teperkis was right to give the same little girl an A+ on the Roman Empire fashion project. That the little girl went on to design collections that made women feel their best.

The meaning of Fotini is light, and it is shining bright for the future.

Stepping into a Bright Future

Evolution is a process.
It is both being and becoming.
—FOTINI

I am writing this from Toronto, where my husband is in good health; my daughter Georgia is now the mother of two beautiful little boys, Mason and Asher, who bring our family great joy; and my youngest Calli has graduated from university, and is following her career path into the wider world. Our darling Bronx, now eleven years old, continues to cuddle and give more love than one can imagine. I adore sharing his feisty, sweet companionship every single day. Our world is never dull. We are all busy with our ever-changing lives.

I am happy to say that my extended family in New York also have full and happy lives, successful as I always knew they would become and remain. I will never lose touch with them, although life gets busy for us all. Many people touched my life in positive ways. And when they didn't, I took away valuable lessons. One never stops learning.

The old saying "Home is where the heart is" could never be simply a greeting card sentiment for me. I have had many homes, traveled far and wide, and learned from experience that the best home is any place filled with love.

Upon my return to Toronto from the demands of the Manhattan fashion industry, I was content to rest and catch my breath. The Romanov Collection was shown here, and I am pleased to say it was received with the highest accolades, reviews, and a standing ovation at the event.

You know me from having read my story. You understand that a routine lifestyle or idleness is not, and never could be, me. No, being captain of many ships is part of who I am and always will be.

But I took my time.

In a sense, I was already doing what I'm doing now. In fact, I had been doing it all my life and then professionally from the time of the Javiera Collection, my design debut. Sometimes the thing you would like most to work at and are best at accomplishing is right in front of you, but you just don't notice it.

The loyalty of my customers and my deep desire to help them be their best selves, to enhance them so they could present their best personal brand to the world was always what gave me the greatest pleasure from collection to collection—from the Latin flair of Javiera to the ancient beauty of Egyptian Queens and Greek Goddesses, from the pastel prettiness of Wisteria of France to the deep, regal richness of the Romanovs. These collections represent not just my art or my skill, but also my soul, who I am.

As a strategic thinker, one who sees the big picture as opposed to what's happening now, I was willing to take my time and allow this evolution to set its own pace—eventually realizing that this was who I have always been and what I have always loved doing. After two years of research, building a business model and strategy for this concept, Personal Brand Enhancement *through fashion* came to fruition.

How could it take so long? Anyone who has ever started a business knows that careful pre-planning is vital. If you start out with a weak business plan, or without keeping your ethics and commitment to others in sight, you are walking on rocky ground and prone to tripping over stumbling blocks. As always, if I was to do something, I wanted it done impeccably and intelligently.

My plan was all-encompassing: to show women how to be the best they can and how to enhance their personal brand through fashion by utilizing the many tools available. My strategy would be to make those tools readily available in several ways and to create a model that would work for every woman, regardless of her goals, body type, or lifestyle.

> *Show women how to be the best they can and how to enhance their personal brand through fashion by utilizing the many tools available.*

First, we secured the services of a marketing and strategy firm with whom we had worked on previous business ventures. The key partners were people who were known for their professionalism and integrity. When we initially embarked, our immediate task was to clarify the concept and tighten the loose ends. This team believed in it, and in me—that was one of the most important factors. During this time, we realized that sharing my own personal and business experiences with other women would be a pivotal move. It would show them that they, too, can design their own path, regardless of their time of life.

Conceptualizing and writing a book was the first action item. Simultaneously, with my vision and some key advisors' counsel, we created a new website, **fotininyc.com**, to let women get help immediately by reading the articles posted. I would like to point out that—as with the FOTINI brand—every supplier and vendor I worked with was carefully sourced. There is no crystal ball to determine when stumbling blocks might appear, but I did my best to avoid some of the challenges I had previously faced in the fashion business. You have to be aligned with your team—it is vital that they believe in you. If they do not, you must let them go.

I prefer to view my website as an online magazine versus a blog. I have the utmost respect for bloggers, but blogging is *not* what I do. My website was designed to take a wide view of subjects pertaining to fashion, lifestyle, and personal growth. The aim is to provide information on a variety of subjects to aspirational women who are starting their journey, as well as successful women determined to stay on top. The website will help all of you reading this book, because it addresses everything from how to gain confidence through fashion and identify your personal brand to developing a routine for success in simple and attainable steps. As important as fashion is in establishing your signature identity, so are self-care and personal growth. In formulating the website, I wanted to make sure it would provide immediate assistance to women who might not be able to come to a talk or book a one-on-one consultation in the near future.

What woman couldn't use some guidance on organizing closets or choosing an unconventional wedding gown? Who wouldn't gain from advice on mentorship and creating a successful capsule wardrobe?

The website also embraces and invites my existing audience and newcomers to get to know me better on a different level than as the designer in this book. Online, as in my talks, I share my day-to-day experiences, and how choices and patterns in life work to reinforce my own personal brand identity.

Through all the planning, I remained true to my vision and aesthetic: not to lecture, judge, or criticize women, but to counsel them and encourage them to put their best selves forward—exactly as I had since that first presentation of my Javiera collection and my debut trunk show in Texas. I kept it personal, because I always present the authentic me so women can see me as I am, a woman like them who wants nothing more than to crawl back under the covers on some days, a woman who questions and strives to improve herself. Growth, after all, is never static; it is an ongoing process that lasts a lifetime.

During that period, even while I was deliberating and designing my new endeavor, I was writing this book. It was a challenge for me: how to craft a memoir that provided an inside look at the exciting but often cutthroat world of the New York fashion industry while at same time sharing my personal and professional journey and the lessons I learned along the way. I hope you agree that I have shared a story of perseverance, discipline, focus, and drive, and that it has inspired you in your own life and work. We *can* have it all—it's just that it doesn't always happen as we planned, and sometimes we can't have it all at the same time. Over the years, I have also defined and prioritized what is most important to me. That comes with time, and we cannot expect be perfect at all times. We are all a work in progress.

We are all a work in progress.

With the new business concept, I decided to do what I am now doing not on a whim or after much soul searching, but because my past and present simply fell into place in the most organic manner. I have never doubted that I am the type of person who needs to keep working, who lacks the desire to be idle, unproductive, or to stop contributing. I am, and always will be, the same determined hard worker I was as child bent over my Barbie sewing machine, the young lady at Merrill Lynch who wanted to conquer the investment banking industry, a budding designer studying corsetry in Italy, and a successful designer relishing every moment of seeing her creations applauded and purchased.

I have always been eager and excited to take my next steps.

It has been a whirlwind of hard work, exhilaration, and rewards in one form or another. I was as busy as I had ever been as a designer, but now I was building a design that covered fashion and beyond, that approached fashion from a new standpoint for others yet was for me an intensified commitment to my lifetime principles of being a confidante and advisor.

If you are starting out or even just dreaming of becoming an entrepreneur, be aware that you are entering a world that requires you to stay healthy, focused, and dedicated, and that it is sometimes lonely. Concurrently, while looking after my family, when I wasn't writing the book, I was writing articles and updating the website. Other times, I was planning and working on photo shoots, podcasts, and videos. And like any consultant, my product was myself, which meant I couldn't and wouldn't hand over everything else and do no more than pose for photos. That's just not who I am. As you all know by now, I am and will remain the captain of my ship. Thankfully, I was prepared. Hadn't I worked around the clock in the New York fashion industry? Hadn't I been making alterations up to moments before a presentation and working on the next season's collection, even as I was in the showroom selling the current one?

This extension of the FOTINI brand is as rewarding as I thought it would be. I am excited to be counseling women on how to identify their personal brand through visual representation. I am seeing women become more confident before my eyes as they make changes—sometimes subtle, sometimes on a larger scale—having discovered they previously hadn't had much of a brand identity of their authentic self or represented themselves in the best possible way.

Everything I have accomplished, every amazing day I have spent working in fashion and working with women throughout North America, has been a privilege for me. I never forget that. I have been fortunate to have my dream career in fashion, the sphere I yearned to be part of for so many years, the industry I love in all its beauty and with all its blemishes. People sometimes say, "Oh, Fotini, you're so lucky!" But it didn't come easily. The most valued things in life, the things that really matter, do not.

No one is going to come knocking on your door offering you your dreams—you have to go after them and earn them with hard work.

> *No one is going to come knocking on your door offering you your dreams—you have to go after them and earn them with hard work.*

No matter what your heart's desire—whether it is to be a teacher, a tech developer, an entertainer, or a designer—you need to make a commitment. You need to strategize and work hard and go after what you want. I have never believed that things *always* happen for a reason. Yes, sometimes a little bit of luck and the right timing can help, but we cannot rely on that. You are the driver of your destiny—as I am of mine, as we all are. Your promise is to yourself and your dream.

I still have the mood boards and sketches from my next fashion collection. The inspiration and designs are timeless and will be relevant whenever I decide to turn them into reality. Day by day, I step into the future. And that future is wide and deep and capable of holding all sorts of marvelous challenges and stirring accomplishments.

New York City had been in my heart and soul for many years

prior to me building my fashion house. It will always have a place there; it is like no other city in the world. I sometimes say, when asked to compare it with another city, that there *is* no other city like it, because it is like a country of its own. The people, pace and diversity, and the excitement of all the dreams that may be possible is intoxicating. For me, it continues to feel like home when I arrive; it has taught and continues to teach me many valuable lessons. I am still working with wonderful people in Manhattan. I may have a better balance of my living arrangements with my base in Toronto, but New York remains and will forever be a part of me, just as my beloved Central Park continues to be one of the best places I have ever found to decompress. If there is a better place to go for a meditative and energizing run, I have yet to discover it.

For now, I continue to evolve, to be my best authentic self, committed to what brought me success, no matter how challenging that can sometimes be. And I continue to find joy and satisfaction in helping other women as they, too, evolve and reach for the sky.

And whenever I look back on that fateful day of September 12, 2011, my first NYFW presentation, it is as if I am experiencing it for the first time. The nervousness; the butterflies in my stomach; the anticipation, excitement, and longing. I see myself as I take the elevator up to the penthouse of the Gramercy Park Hotel for the debut of my Javiera Collection. I was that collection, and every collection that followed. Each collection was me.

And the elevator doors opened and it all began.

Now, as I close my eyes, I am there once more, stepping off the elevator onto the lush burgundy carpet. I watch as the crew transforms this beautiful penthouse into a stage for my designs. I feel anew the nervousness and excitement of that triumphant day when the FOTINI brand officially arrived.

What began in that suite continues. The joy of it lives on.

Today, I am being and becoming. And for that little girl on the veranda, the light keeps shining through.

ABOUT THE AUTHOR

Fotini Copeland is a personal brand enhancement consultant, inspiring and advising women on how to enhance their own brand through fashion.

In 2007, Fotini spent three years traveling in Italy and studying the construction of corsetry—her design passion—beside old-world ateliers in Bologna, Como, and Bergamo. In 2010, she founded FOTINI, her New York-based fashion design house with her luxury ready-to-wear brand at the forefront. She showcased her first of five collections at New York Fashion Week in 2012, and later at Houston Fashion Week. Her collections reflected femininity and strength through a realistic and wearable approach to fashion—a woman designing for women.

This new business venture of the FOTINI brand came organically. A natural conversationalist, Fotini found that women turned to her as an advisor and confidante. Using her unmatched fashion, design, and lifestyle expertise, she has assisted numerous women in telling their stories through their personal brand. Her focus is on matters relating to fashion, demeanor, design, and expression capability—to inspire women to be the best version of themselves.

MORE FROM FOTINI

www.fotininyc.com

facebook.com/FOTINInyc

Instagram: fotininyc

Twitter: @Fotininyc